To Julia + Charlie
With all my love
[signature]

A Way

The Story of a Long Walk

A Way

The Story of a Long Walk
Jenna Smith

Urban Loft Publishers | Portland, Oregon

A Way
The Story of a Long Walk

Urban Loft Publishers
2034 NE 40th Avenue #414
Portland, OR 97212
www.theurbanloft.org

ISBN-13: 978-1496054142
ISBN-10: 1496054148

Made in the U.S.A.

Cover art and map of the road by Maxime Girard.

Names and details of people have been changed to protect privacy of individuals

This book is dedicated to Nicolas Croze-Orton who pushed and prodded me forward every step of the way with the tip of his walking stick.

Table of Contents

Book One: France

Book Two: Spain

Map of the Road

Foreword
Gordon MacDonald

My introduction to Jenna Smith came about 20 years ago while visiting her home. I recall a shy, smallish girl who took her violin very seriously and who—on that day—was looking forward to listening to the Metropolitan Opera on the radio. Opera! Really?

I remember that Jenna, the teenager, was "teaseable," that it was not hard to get her giggling as we bantered back and forth about matters I hoped might be of interest to her. Jenna's confidence to look an adult, a stranger at that, in the eye and engage in conversation caused me to say to myself, "You'll hear a lot more from this girl in days to come."

One of those days has come, and it's my privilege to introduce Jenna Smith to you. Jenna the walker, Jenna, the woman of deepening spirit and mind, Jenna the exceptionally good author.

It was Jenna's father—a close friend—who told me one day that his daughter and her husband, Nicolas, were preparing to make the St. James Pilgrimage in Europe during the summer of 2011. They would start in France, he said, and end in Santiago di Compostella, Spain, a walking distance of approximately 1,000 miles.

I was vaguely acquainted with the Camino (as it is more popularly called), wishing that one day I might walk it myself. So I said, "When they get on their way, keep me in touch with every step of their journey." He did.

Jenna insists that writing this book was not the purpose of that walk. I believe her. No, the reason for the walk was personal: simply to walk … and to let whatever experiences, whatever people, and whatever questions she encountered worm their ways into one's heart. I get that.

A walk or a journey—such as the St. James Pilgrimage—is often used as a metaphor for life. It's not difficult to recall any number of books in which a journey has been the platform for what an author wants to say.

Homer's *Odyssey*, is a good example. The Bible offers us Abraham's journey from his birthplace to Canaan. Then there is Israel's latter journey (Moses, the leader) to the Promised Land. Later, there would be Chaucer's *Canterbury Tales*. I suppose that Bunyan's *Pilgrim's Progress* ought also to make this quick list.

The 18th and 19th centuries gave us a treasure trove of books about exploration and discovery which I think meet the general criteria of the metaphor of journey. There are also the great stories of the settlers who moved across the plains of Canada and the United States, and finally there are the amazing journeys of astronauts to the moon and, soon, beyond. Two more modern books that jog my memory are John Updike's *Travels with Charlie* and Bill Bryson's *A Walk in the Woods* (painfully funny).

When a boy, I was romanced by a popular song that went like this. "Faraway places with strange sounding names/Faraway over the sea/ Those far away places with their strange sounding names/calling, calling me." The song touched a deep longing in me to travel. But not just to travel. To see things; meet people; enlarge meaning. Experience the world God had given to us.

And that urging brings me back to Jenna Smith's *A Way*. Because, in her book, she has gone to faraway places and come to enrich us with her unique look at life in journey-form.

Jenna dares to offer us her heart. She is not squeamish in giving us a vivid description of what a woman is likely to face during a 1,000-mile walk. The title itself warns of what might come. Things which some times fall below the romantic standard. Tough things, painful things, invidious things.

Is there a question any of us might want to ask that Jenna does not offer to honestly answer? Is there exhaustion, sickness, irritability, fear, loss of spirit on the Camino. Yes. Does one have to deal with marital tension, embarrassing hygiene issues, strange and tasteless people? Of course. Would one ever wish to quit, admit defeat, wonder if God has anything to do with this insane attempt to walk these distances? You bet.

But having addressed these issues more than once, Jenna Smith offers a higher view of life on the Camino. She describes the way love between a husband and wife can enlarge. How friendships can form with people one might never engage with in other circumstances. Jenna thinks out loud (and not always reverently) about the place of busyness, material things, even organized religion in our lives. And all of this is just a scratch on the surface of a delightful book that touches upon so many of those issues each of us thinks about and wonders about with such regularity.

Honestly? I doubt that I shall ever walk the Camino—even if I fanaticize about doing it—but, thanks to Jenna Smith, I think I have been there ... at least in my imagination. Not only have I seen what she has seen (the beauty, the antiquity, the spiritual), but I have mused on core themes of human experience and been spiritually nourished.

Thank you, Jenna ... and welcome to the world of authorship. *A Way* is not your last book.

Gordon MacDonald
Chancellor, Denver Seminary
Concord, New Hampshire

Foreword

Preface

As soon as I began walking, I began writing. It's as simple as that.

May 12, 2011, was half-sunny, half-rainy when my husband, Nicolas, and I took our first steps out of the town of Le-Puy-en-Velay in southern France onto the road that would somehow lead us all the way to Santiago di Compostella, on Spain's Atlantic coast. I had a paper journal with me, completely blank save for a few important emergency numbers and the addresses of loved ones jotted down on the front page. When we took our first break of the day, around the second hour of walking, I pulled out the journal and began writing.

And so it began. For the rest of the journey, when we stopped in churches, I jotted down their names, the saints who were venerated there, and the inscriptions on the walls. At night after supper, I wrote down the town we were in and what we ate. I recorded conversations, transcribed recipes, listed the animals that crossed our paths. And then I thought a little bit about my day, and wrote down all of that, too. I emailed family and friends, trying to add some humor about the quirky people, the hole-in-the-wall places we passed through, so that the recipients would be entertained while following our journey, and I saved my letters.

That's how this book came to be. It wasn't so much that I wrote a memoir of my pilgrimage. Rather, the writing was part of the pilgrimage. It became as much a part of the road as putting on my ridiculously expensive socks every morning. When we tried new food that I had never heard of before, I thought, "I have to figure out what these ingredients are and write them down." When we arrived at our half-way mark, in Saint-Jean-Pied-de-Port, while everyone headed over to the outdoor store to stock up on sunscreen, ponchos, and better footgear, I went over to the stationery store and bought myself a new pen. I didn't do the Camino in order to write a book. But writing a book wound up enriching my experience as a pilgrim and accompanying me all the way through.

What you will find in its contents is somewhat a story, somewhat a collection of essays. It has a narrative arc covering the entire journey. But there are several chapters scattered throughout that leave the boundaries of time and space. These chapters, such as "The Price of Beauty" or "The Body," are my reflections that were born out of the experience of my walk.

Nothing in this book was meant to be an academic contribution, theological or otherwise. But if its content appears theological or philosophical, that is because of my years as a graduate student in theology. Theological reflection is part of who I am. The book has neither the research nor the rigor that a theological project would require, but if its basic principles and reflections could inspire a scholar, a reader or an amateur to venture further into the exploration of the themes found in this book, then so be it.

It was not either intended to be a "Christian" book or a "Spiritual" book, but I will not deny that many of its themes, conversations and reflections reflect Christian worldviews. I am a Christian, and the pilgrimage of Saint-James was born out of Christendom, so writing a book about this road without mentioning the Christian faith would be like reading a sailor's memoir who forgot to mention the sea. Again, the thoughts, observations or anecdotes pertaining to Christianity, its institutions, rituals or practices are not really the result of any rigorous research. They are all born out of my life experiences, and my perceptions of things.

Finally, to all those potential pilgrims out there: I hope this story inspires you, moves you, and maybe even give you the courage to bite the bullet and book those plane tickets to France or Spain or India or

Patagonia or wherever it is you were planning your great adventure. But please, promise me this: don't use my story as a guidebook. My experiences need not be your experiences, my itinerary need not be your itinerary. Mine is but one account, not a how-to manual on doing the Saint-James Way. We all need to figure out our own journeys. If we set out with too many expectations or preconceptions we may be disappointed. I have met many disappointed pilgrims. And on the flip side, don't be scared. It's not because I wound up flea-bitten, constipated and dehydrated, puking my guts out in a hospital room in Galicia that this need be your fate. Some people do the Camino and wind up just fine, without a scratch—Scout's honor! So happy reading, and take a hike!

Preface

Acknowledgements

A book is not a solo project, even if it is a solitary one. Many people came together to make first the trip, and then the book, a reality. Nicolas, first and foremost: patron saint of financial planning, expert lost sock locator, motivator of discouraged walkers, and generally the most patient of partners, you continually amaze me. My parents: my father is the best cheerleader a girl could ever want and my mother is the editor extraordinaire. Their support made it all happen. The staff and board of Christian Direction and Innovation Youth made my sabbatical possible, and for that I am eternally grateful. My friends and my siblings cared for Leo the cat while we were away, humored us while we rambled on and on and on about the pilgrimage and sat through a few slide shows. That is true friendship. They even forgave me when they found out only after the signing of the publisher's contract that I had actually written a book. To Christa Smith, Julia Smith-Brake, Charlie Smith-Brake, Marie-France Boisvert, Alexandre Gregoire, Marie-Ève Fortier, Patrick Laurin, Jacynthe Vaillancourt, Willemijn de Groot, Martin Grenier, Geoffrois Psaila, Geneviève Parent, Beth Neelin-Robinson, Catherine Riberdy St-Pierre, Tran-Quan Luong, Christiane Croze and Grandpa Smith, thank you all for being a part of my life.

Thanks to Anne St-Hilaire, the godmother of Compostelle, and the team of Québec à Compostelle and La Tienda.

The Friends Meeting of Montreal and the parish of St. Stephen's Anglican: thanks for being as loving as you are.

Acknowledgements

To all the people I met on the road: I would never have written this had it not been for you. Or at least, the book wouldn't have been half as good without you. Your presence, conversations, stories and friendship blessed me. I remember your faces and your words so much more than any village, meal or church. You were the road. Thank you.

Finally, the biggest thanks go out to Sean Benesh and all the crew at Urban Loft Publishers. This project was a step outside the box, and I am deeply appreciative for the opportunity.

Glossary of Terms

Albergue: Inn, in Spanish

Buen Camino: A Spanish greeting, meaning have a good road

Camino: The Way, in Spanish

Café con leche: Coffee with milk

Le Chemin: Literally, the road in French

Hospitaleros: Hosts, most commonly used for hosts in inns or refuges for pilgrims

Pèlerin/Pèlerine: French term for pilgrim (masculine and feminine)

Peregrino/Peregrina: Spanish term for pilgrim (masculine and feminine)

Refugio: A refuge, most commonly less expensive than a hotel and run by a monastery or municipality

Saint-Jacques de Compostelle: Saint James of Compostella in French

Santiago di Compostella: Saint James of Compostella in Spanish

Glossery of Terms

Introduction

Every year thousands of people undertake the pilgrimage of Saint James, most commonly referred to as the Camino. In French, we usually say Compostelle, because Santiago di Compostella (the Cathedral of Saint James in Galicia, Spain) is the final destination. The modern road most walked towards Santiago is called the Camino Frances (the French Way), because during the Middle Ages it was the road the French pilgrims would use, starting in the Pyrenees and traversing all the way through northern Spain towards the Atlantic coast.

There are many roads that lead to Santiago, many Caminos, if you will. In France alone there are four or five itineraries that lead into Spain. Portugal has a path, the Camino Portuguès, and Spain has several, some going inland (such as the Via Plata), another one tracing the upper coastline (the Camino del Norte). We met one person who had walked all the way from Holland, another from Austria, and we heard of one person who had walked all the way from Moscow. It turns out that all of Europe has roads whose destination is Santiago di Compostella. This is a very old pilgrimage, as Saint James' tomb was discovered in AD 813. A first version of the church of Santiago was built around 840, and pilgrims began their journeys around the tenth century. The tradition of walking the Camino was greatly aided throughout the Middle Ages as different monastic orders, notably the Templars of Jerusalem, set up hospitals and inns along the Camino, hosting and healing pilgrims.

For centuries this was a strictly religious pilgrimage, reserved for those doing penance or for priests and nobility wishing to pay homage to the shrine of Saint James, the brother of John the Evangelist, one of the twelve apostles. This was not a very popular trek, with barely more than a few hundred people doing it every year. But in the twentieth century, the European Union put a great deal of money and energy into popularizing the pilgrimage, making it more accessible with better road markers (usually a scallop seashell, emblem of Saint James), municipal inns, pilgrim passports (called Credencials, to be stamped at every village you stop in), and rerouting certain itineraries so that pilgrims would have better choices of towns to stay in.

Santiago di Compostella was host in 1989 to World Youth Day and Pope John Paul II, which gave the pilgrimage renewed international attention.

We are no doubt in an era of Camino revival, as the number of pilgrims each year increases. In 2012, nearly 200,000 people received a Compostella, a certificate for their pilgrimage. On a Holy Year (whenever July 25, the anniversary of Saint James, falls on a Sunday), the numbers will go up. Purists will complain about the numbers of people on the road, but in my experience, large numbers were never really an issue, except for the last three or four days before reaching Santiago. The number of pilgrims who receive a certificate of accomplishment in no way reflects the number of people actually on the road at any given point. Also, the further away from Santiago you begin, the fewer people you'll find on the Camino. We began in Puy-en-Velay, in France, some 1,000 miles from our final destination. We encountered only small pockets of people walking at any given point.

Most pilgrims walk with their bags on their back. Everything you will need for your pilgrimage you carry with you. It gives new meaning to the term "essentials." Villages, towns and farms are set up to accommodate pilgrims along the way as part of an inn or bed-and-breakfast system. In France, you normally pay a set price to the host for a bed, an evening meal and breakfast. In Spain, it is a bit less regimented. You usually pay for the price of your room and grab your meals at the café or bar. Some towns had three or four choices of places to stay, but the smaller the town, the less choice you had. This is how you wind up meeting your fellow pilgrims. Everyone walks at their own pace during the day, but meet up to wine and dine together in the evenings and mornings. Hospitality and communal eating are pillars of this pilgrimage.

Finally, there are people from all walks of life, all with their own motivations for undertaking a Camino. There are still many people who do it as an expression of their religious beliefs, while some even do the walk for the most traditional reasons, such as giving thanks for an answered prayer or a blessing, or to do penance. But for most people, if there is a spiritual motivation behind their walk, it normally has to do with soul-searching, or building a bridge towards a life change. For many, this has become a cultural walk, whether it be an alternative way to experience Europe and history, or as a means of keeping their love of hiking or exercise alive while walking through more than just woods or mountains.

History, culture, diverse motivations, all these elements make up what we call the Way. Buen Camino!

Introduction

Book 1
France

Prelude
I Walk

So many people, before, during and after the Camino asked me why I was doing this pilgrimage. To this day I still have a hard time giving a clear answer. I could say it was a spiritual quest, and in a certain way it was, but it wasn't really that direct. I already had acquired, or at least admired, the values of journeying, of solitude, community and simplicity. I didn't leave to recover from a bad divorce, or some tragic death in my life or to radically change my lifestyle. I am the director of an inner-city youth center. It's not like I had to do a pilgrimage to release myself from a dog-eat-dog career in the stock market or corporate law. I wasn't trying to find my soul mate—I had already found him. I wasn't escaping, because there aren't enough bad things in my life that needed escaping from. In the end, mine is an altogether boring story of picking up my bags and walking. But walk I do.

It's cold, I walk. It's too hot, I walk. I have my period, and still I walk. My feet hurt, my eyes are tired, my muscles fatigued, my neck is sore. The bag is heavy. Still I walk. If I haven't had enough sleep, I walk. I have walked through thunderstorms, drenched to the bone, lifting a hand to brush back my hair and feeling ice-cold water run down my arm to my chest. I've walked through plains and fields of poppies and wheat, and green meadows and vineyards, on soft mossy ground and hard scorching asphalt. I've seen the sunrise over the road and walked until the evening sky sets in. I say goodbye to pilgrims who have reached their destination and continued walking with a heavy heart, feeling just a little more alone. I've walked in silence. I've walked through noise. I've talked to people while walking non-stop for eight hours. The next day, I'll be alone, with Nic half a mile ahead of me. I'll walk in silence again. I receive news of my grandfather's ailing health, sure to pass away before I'll see him again, and still I will walk. I have a feeling of dread, of boredom, telling myself as I wake up, no, not another day. But I walk anyways.

And then come the mornings when I wake up wanting to walk. This is the nicest time, when the desire scoops me up and plants my twitching legs on the ground as if the earth were my glove. The walking isn't a bridge to my life's lesson. The walking is the lesson.

So why did I walk 1,056 miles from France to Spain through wind and rain and hail, you ask? Well, first of all, I just like to walk.

Chapter 1
Why?

There was never a really big carved-out reason to do the Saint James pilgrimage. Coming from Quebec, a land of avid outdoorsy walkers with a tortured history of codependence on the Catholic Church, we'd heard plenty about it. My husband, Nicolas, and I knew we wanted to do it together; we had talked about even before getting married several years earlier. Nicolas' godfather had talked to us many times about it, mourning the fact that his touch-and-go health never allowed him to do it. We got to our fifth wedding anniversary and realized that within the next year we would both have completed our university studies, we'd be somewhat financially stable—not enough to have any sex appeal to a real estate agent but a notch higher than our days as students living off canned tuna. We didn't have children, and I had bargained with my work to take a short sabbatical in lieu of a pay raise. We figured that we'd talked long enough about doing the pilgrimage, so now we were in a place that begged the question, "Why not?" rather than "Why?" So in an act that defied building up our assets and long-term financial planning, we bought a pair of plane tickets and began the preparations.

Once the decision was made, and the tickets bought, I felt happy to know that I could pick up and do something out of the ordinary.

Not that my life was empty or boring. I was approaching 30, settling down into a steady career in community work. We had an urban yuppy lifestyle. We lived near downtown, went to our favorite pub once a week, supported a local independent café with all our pocket money, we recycled and composted. We voted (leftist, of course), exercised (sort of), knit (me, not him), paid taxes (reluctantly), and bought designer shoe wear (see knitting status).

There wasn't a reason in the world not to be content with our lives and yet once we knew we were going on the Camino, I was absolutely thrilled to throw myself into something that would swoop me out of normalcy, knowing that there wasn't just stressful work and outings on the town awaiting me over the next couple of months. I went to every baby shower and house warming and felt truly happy for all parties involved. But my mind was somewhere else. It was on the trail.

We were told by the members of our regional pilgrim's association, Québec à Compostelle, that there are three voyages that you go on when you decide to do "Compostelle", as they call it in French. The voyage of preparation, the actual walk, and then the post-pilgrimage, the one you are on when you return.

The voyage of preparation began as soon as we decided to go, which was a full year before we actually left. Hardly a day went by that I didn't think about what it would be like, didn't imagine myself walking on some long desert road, didn't take a peek into our tour guide book and look at what villages we'd be passing through: villages that no one had ever heard of and no one would ever take much interest in, but that we would be walking through, sleeping in, stopping at their center square to fill up our water canteens. We'd be seeing Europe from a perspective that few ever do.

You couldn't find a better researcher than Nicolas. For a full year he enthusiastically read books, magazines, Internet articles, signed us up for walks with our association, and talked virtually to every hiking amateur or sports equipment expert he could find. Within a short and frightfully expensive period of time we had gone to every outdoor sports store in our vicinity and bought equipment for every stop along the way. "We'll have to go now," he began saying, "or else we'll look kinda stupid with all this expensive stuff sitting in our closet."

Indeed, it wasn't all the talking, planning or even the plane tickets that sealed the deal on the actual trip. Nor was it the promises of spiritual enlightenment, personal development and friendships that you make. It was the foot-long bills for all the crap we needed to bring with us. It gave new meaning to the expression "Less is More." It seemed the less you want to carry on you back, the more cold hard cash you have to plunk down in order to attain that level of simplicity.

I began to feel numb at the check-out line as the cashier would say things like, "So we've got three pairs of underwear and four rubber ends for your walking poles ... That'll be $117, please."

Speaking of salespeople, every single one had an opinion, and was ready to throw you out of the store should you question it. "Shoes? Get the sturdy ones, tight around the ankles, heavy soles, that's the trick. You need them to be solid, because your terrain is woodsy and steep."

The next one had the opposite idea: "Shoes? No, no, you want the light ones, the road is flat there, so a nice arch, but ankle support is not necessary. You need your feet to breathe!" And so on. The problem is, I later found out, that the road is at times steep and woodsy, sometimes hard and flat, so it really was all fair game. I have a friend getting ready to do the Camino herself and she opted for hiking shoes instead of boots and the salesperson all but blocked her access to the cash register, he was so convinced that boots were the way to go. "He really ripped into me," she shuddered. "I just wanted the shoes. They go better for me."

Then you would meet what I discovered were a particular breed called the snubbers, whom I found typically hanging around the merino wool section. It's hard to imagine that someone who considered armpit hair on a girl and pooing outdoors pleasing could possibly be an elitist, but life is full of oxymorons and the hiking world is no exception. "Compostelle? Honestly, I wouldn't do Compostelle, because everyone does Compostelle, and you just have to put up with all the people. Honestly, when I hike I need to be alone in the environment. Close to the earth." To be fair, not everyone does Compostelle. Quebec sends about 2,000 people a year to do various bits and pieces of the roads. So fine, there are a lot of people who walk the Camino, but still, it's not exactly a circus parade.

I started to tell her that I thought people were part of the experience. "Yeah, but you've got hikers who really weren't ready for the trip and they're just out there, whining, ruining it for the rest. No. I need for my trails to be original, unique, you know? Like when I was in Thailand. No one knew about that road. Now that was a real hike."

"Have you ever been to Oka?" I ask, thinking about the trails about 40 minutes from downtown Montreal.

She stared at me. "What are you talking about?"

"Never mind." Snubbers typically will search to the ends of the earth for that "perfect piece of trail" but often not even be aware of the beautiful spots in their own backyard.

I began walking. And walking and walking and walking. I walked to work every day instead of taking public transport. Nic and I walked along the river near our apartment, we walked the Mount Royal in the center of Montreal. We walked when we went camping. My legs began to pull me out of bed and want to walk. If I didn't go for a long walk at least once every few days, I felt them twitch and get restless, like a puppy who's been indoors for too long. The walking became my promise of something to come. When I walked, I knew this was my Camino premonition.

We talked to everyone we could get in touch with about what to bring, what to expect. We went to information sessions given by physiotherapists and nurses on how to prevent tendinitis. We talked to returning pilgrims about what items should be in our bags. We listened to testimonies and stories about the great experiences ahead. We watched YouTube clips, looked up the villages on Google maps, read guide books, bought travel magazines. We were convinced that we were well-read, well-prepared, ready to face the road pilgrims.

Three days into the trek, we thought otherwise, as we slogged through muddy roads, with wind beating against our faces, rain freezing our skin and hair. My raincoat was wrong, my bag too heavy, my muscles unfit.

About one week into the Camino, our new friend Célia asked us what we had done to prepare for the trip. Had we gone on hikes? Joined a gym? "Well," I replied, thinking about the stores, and the research and the walking, and the training and the books. "I guess there isn't really anything that actually prepares you for Compostelle, now is there?"

But even in the beginning days, when my equipment felt awkward and the road hurt me like a new pair of hard leather shoes, the question WHY came back. And I would just reply, "We're here. And very content that we are."

Why?

Chapter 2
Day One

It is said that starting your Camino from Le-Puy-en-Velay in France is one of the most richly significant experiences for the pilgrim. Hardly any road is so old, so travelled and so meaningful. Every morning the Cathedral of Le Puy holds its Pilgrim's Mass and the priest blesses each new herd of walkers.

Some will walk for two weeks. Some, like us, will walk for 70 days, and not stop until they arrive at the end of the end—Finistere, the coast town that is three day's walk past Santiago di Compostella. Some will suffer greatly; a few might even die. One may make a life-altering decision, while another may decide to make peace with a great tragedy. One may be trying to get away from it all, while another may be trying to find it all.

There are a thousand different reasons and motivations for starting out, but chances are even the non-religious pilgrim leaving from Le Puy will probably join in the 8:30 a.m. Mass at the Cathedral to receive a blessing. Afterwards, the priest will walk to the front doors and open them to the sunlight. From there, the celebrants will take their first steps onto the French Chemin. The road begins.

Or so I'm told. I never went to the Mass myself. I was in bed recuperating from a sleepless night due to an unbelievably loud snorer in our room. When we'd arrived at the inn the previous night, the host asked us if we minded semi-private accommodations. Of course we didn't, we replied, we didn't expect to have our own room every night. Mixed dormitories are a common occurrence in the culture of the Camino. But having better foresight, I would have paid our innkeeper whatever he asked and taken the private bedroom. This man sleeping next to us could wake the dead. I do declare my mattress may have shook. Not only were his snores deafening, they were also incessant. I could not have had more than 30 minutes of uninterrupted sleep all night.

Did I bring along ear plugs, you ask?

My dear readers, when a man not four feet away is inhaling so deeply that you could swear there was a SAWMILL lodged in his esophagus, earplugs are of no avail. Would you use scotch tape to protect your house from a tsunami? My point exactly.

All this to say that I woke up the morning of our first day of walking still jetlagged from the trip over and completely sleep-deprived thanks to Ol' Chainsaw one bed over. Also, I was still suffering from a stress cold that started back in Montreal, no doubt brought on by the hectic preparations for our Camino sabbatical and the recent federal Conservative Party's majority win. We were facing Day One of the walk and I was groggy, grumpy and congested.

Nic sighed and rubbed his eyes, looking hung-over. I am half hoping he'll say, "Go back to sleep, we'll walk tomorrow."

"The Mass is in 20 minutes," he says, looking at his watch.

"I'm too cranky to go to a freakin' Mass."

"Fair enough."

We opt to grab a bite to eat and hit the road.

There is a lot that's blurry about our entire 70-day walk—names of villages, days of the week, what church we saw where. But I do clearly remember setting out on the first day. I remember putting down our first step and taking a picture of it. I remember how happy Nicolas was. This trip was the fruit of his efforts, much more than of mine. I remember feeling like one part of the trip—the planning and waiting part—was already over. The first step came as a relief: we're here, we can start. We'd put so much into the preparation that I had begun to feel a little paranoid that some great stroke of bad luck would befall us—like a broken leg a week before the beginning of the walk—and we'd have to delay or cancel the whole thing. But this didn't happen, and we were starting out. No great obstacle could stop us now from doing this.

We read our first sign: "Saint-Jacques-de-Compostelle—1,497 km" with its famous seashell emblem of the pilgrimage.

Nic frowned. "I could have sworn it was longer than that." I shrugged. We walked for 15 minutes. Second sign, this time carved into an official European Union stone marker, said, "Saint-Jacques-de-Compostelle—1,698 km."

I gasped. "So let me get this right. We've been walking for 15 minutes and have just added something like 125 miles onto our trajectory?"

Nic howled. "The first post must be the historical one. The European Union redid all the markings in 2001. This is the accurate one."

So ... on Day One, I am recovering from a cold and jetlag, haven't slept a wink, and the road just became 125 miles longer. And we're off.

Then it began to pour. A light drizzle at first, and then a great downpour. The bottom of my pant legs got sprayed and stained with mud. I look at Nic. "Very appropriate."

We walked. Sloshed, more like it. And huffed and panted as we ascended to different levels of the forestry road. We looked at cows, a great many of them. We smiled and nodded at other walkers, some of whom we would never see again, others whom we would see over and over again for weeks to come.

"Bonjour!" I hear a cheery voice behind me. Our first meeting with Marius. Marius was from Switzerland and had already been walking 45 days. He'd started his journey in Geneva. We introduce ourselves and his eyes twinkle.

He cheerfully exclaims, "Des petits québecois!" (Little Quebeckers!), as he stops to talk to us at our first break of the day (the first of many, I might add). He peers into our lunch bag. "You packed too much food. It will weigh down your pack, putting too much weight on your hips, which may in time cause tendinitis. Tendinitis could slow you down, even make you stop your walk for two, maybe three days. Best get rid of extra weight." He says this all in the most cheerful of tones. "Later!" And with that, he giggles and saunters off.

We eat our lunch quietly. My pace is slow. I am normally a strong walker at home, doing a bit more than 3 miles an hour, which is far from speed-walking but decent for a short person. Here, I'm slow. It may be my bag, or fatigue, or maybe my mind can't get into sync with my body. But whatever it is, I'm lagging behind Nic. The sun comes out and burns our faces so that by the time we arrive at the inn that night, our clothes are wet and our skin burnt by the sun. By the end of Day One, we had walked eight hours up and down, over rocks and roots, around trees, with backpacks that are too heavy, feet too untrained and spirits too tired. Marius crosses us a few times giggling the whole way. He's nearly three times my age and could seemingly out-walk me in his sleep.

I am on the verge of discouragement, but then, there's a bend in the road and we cross over a tiny bridge with a picturesque cottage and watermill on the other side. I half expect to see Snow White and the Seven Dwarves come out and greet me. Nicolas points to a sign. "Jen," he says, "Look." The sign reads "Saint-Privat-d'Allier." We're at the end of our first stretch of road. It's all I can do to keep from crying. Marius peeks his head out from the inn. "Mes petits québécois! You made it. How stupendous. Come in, I have a bottle of wine with your names on it."

At supper, with several other pilgrims that we met here and there on the road, we eat a three-course meal and down two bottles of wine. People recommend various French movies to each other, judge each other's choices of socks and rain gear and complain about the new smoking bans in cafés and restaurants. We compare the weight in our bags and try out Marius' bag-to-human weight ratio and decide that we have all over-packed. I am tired but uplifted.

Day One is over.

Day One

Chapter 3
Bruce and Lucy

We were warned. Day two would be five hundred meters up, five hundred meters down. Thank God for a full night's sleep. The staff at La Cabourne in Saint-Privat-d'Allier gave us a room for two. Nic and I slept in so much that by the time we lugged ourselves down for breakfast, everyone else in the place had left, leaving nothing but bread crumbs and coffee stains on the table cloths. "Wow," I said, "Marius is gone? And Célia? We really are like the teens on the road." The cook walked in and laughed when she saw us, "Ah, les jeunes!" (Oh, the young ones!) We look at her sheepishly. She shakes her head and says, "Don't worry, I will get you some orange juice." She made us promise to send her a picture once we'd arrived in Santiago di Compostella.

And we were off. Saint-Privat-d'Allier is the type of village you would imagine in a French fairytale. It is literally nestled into sharp rocky mountains, which looks adorable in photographs but makes you sweat and curse upon its entry and exit.

It didn't take five minutes of walking before we were nearly rock climbing our way out of town. "Man," I pant, "I feel like I need an ice pick." Eventually, we climbed down. And down and down and down. "Hmm," I think to myself near the end of the afternoon as we sit on a water trough. "What's that sharp point I feel on my toe?"

I peel my sock off. My first blister.

Blisters are to the Camino what acne is to adolescence. A blessed few undeservedly escape that fate, but a good many are seemingly cursed and must endure the unpleasantness for as long as the gods so wish. I have soft, sensitive skin on my feet. This is a sweet way of saying it tears, bleeds, chafes, blisters and scabs and generally looks like ground meat by the end of a hike or after I wear a pair of adorable open-toed stylish sandals on a hot day.

This first blister—let's call him Bruce—wraps himself intelligently around my big toe from the nail diagonally down to the pad, so that over the next few days I would be virtually incapable of ever getting the bandage quite right, which means that it would take forever to heal. I would get a couple of days of respite and then, Bang! As soon as we would hit a good descent, Bruce would be right back on top of his game, swelling up, sometimes hiding a second layer of liquid under him. In clinical terms, we could call this a blister within a blister, or in other words, hiker hell.

Bruce was not alone. Three hours later, when we arrived at the inn, I peeled off my sock and found another one underneath my pinkie toe. Let's call her Lucy. Lucy reared her ugly face on that second day, but would reincarnate and haunt me for the remainder of my time in France, 30 days in all.

Lucy was a bitch.

Flaky, undecided, manipulative, deceitful and just plain mean. I would put hours of care into her, tending to her sweetly, softly, bathing her in warm water and disinfectant, buying her the prettiest and most expensive bandages, bending over backwards at her every beck and call. All to no avail. I would wrap her up but she was just always changing her mind.

"There," I would say to her. "I pulled the band-aid tight, just like you asked."

"Yeah" she would reply nonchalantly, "but today, I'm feeling sweaty, so the band-aid will probably fall off. Better put some cotton on it."

"Ok, Luce, but no more requests after this."

"Yeah ..." Lucy would shrug her shoulders, "The thing is, I'm not feeling the cotton. Better put the moleskin on it...hmm, I don't like that either...did you hear me? I don't like it, I don't like it, HEY!!" And then she would fill with liquid again, turn red and send me running for the hills. If I could run for the hills, that is, which I couldn't, because, you know, I had blisters.

The French enjoy talking about blisters almost as much as they enjoy talking about wine. It seems to be a favorite topic of conversation over the apéritif, or so I discover that evening of our second day. I sit down at the picnic table, greeting our fellow walkers, and Marius, our new Swiss friend peers over my foot. "Ah, ma petite québecoise! Il vous faut de la bé-ta-di-ne," he said cheerfully. (O my little Quebecker! You need iodine.)

"Et des compides!" piped in Chantal. Compides. If I heard that word once, I heard it a thousand times. The collective lot of French hikers was a walking, breathing advertisement for les compides. They are basically a thick, latex-free, cushiony bandage that they would place over the potential wound or unopened blister. Nothing, not sweat, not a shower, not a nuclear explosion could tear it off its place. Seven days seems to have been the record for it staying in place and even then, you needed to pry it off the skin with a certain amount of force.

There were two problems that I had with the infamous compides. One, Lucy-the-pinkie-blister, didn't like them. They squeezed her too much and created unnecessary pressure, causing the toe to feel uncomfortable and painful. Two, I had to mortgage my house to pay for a box of ten. Well, that last statement may have been the teeniest bit of an exaggeration, but by my second trip to the pharmacy in less than three days, Nicolas and I began rethinking our Camino budget. "Your blisters are adding new meaning to the term 'hidden expense,'" he sighs.

Back to our inn. As I sit at the picnic table between Nic and Marius, the minute I show off my feet I had approximately five overly curious faces surrounding my foot, every one of them blurting out the most knowledgeable and experienced opinions.

"Keep it completely uncovered, it needs to air out."

"Non, non, non, you must pierce it and then wash it and cover it up."

"Pierce it? Non, non, non, she cannot pierce it, she must leave it alone!"

"She must pierce it, for she needs to walk on it tomorrow."

"Merde!"

"Psst!" I hear someone calling to me. I turn around and see a jolly face smiling at me, peace earrings dangling down to her shoulders. "Hi, honey. Let me look at your feet." She had an American accent.

I raise my blistered foot. She sucks in her breath. "Eesh. You've some blood there. You want my daughter to look at it? She's been taking care of her blisters for the past hour. And she's a nurse."

I nod and follow her into her bedroom.

"Kit? We've got another one." A thin, blond woman peeks out from the bathroom. "Come on in! I hear you're Canadian?"

"Yup."

"We're from Seattle. Well, I am. Mom's been living in Lebanon for the past couple of years. This is our yearly two-week getaway. Good grief, mom, why didn't we just take a trip to Hawaii?"

"Oh, Kit." Her mother looks at me. "Old waterworks here bawled for about twenty minutes when we arrived today at the inn."

Kit gives her a warning look. "Mom, today's been tough." She shows me her toes.

"Ouch!" I exclaim. "I thought mine were bad."

"Yeah, well, here's what I've been doing. French trick. You take the needle and thread, soak them in iodine and then thread the blister. Keep the string in so that it drains but doesn't open up the blister."

I look at her with morbid curiosity. "Does it work?"

"Well, most people swear by it. Wanna try?"

"Let's do it."

She threads Bruce first and I watch the liquid pour out. "Oooooooh!" Her mother is covering her eyes and scrunching her face. "I can't bear it!"

"It looks like this is worse for you than for me," I laugh.

"I'm a mother."

"OK," I say a bit faintly, feeling the iodine go into the sore. "I think I'll just put up my feet. Quite literally. Thanks for helping me. This has been the most memorable of first encounters."

The two laugh. "My name is Jane," says her mother.

"Jenna."

"Well, honey, just come back if you need anything else popped."

"I might just take you up on that offer." I limp out on the heels of my feet, trying not to disturb the strings hanging off of my toes, leaving a trail of brownish iodine liquid behind me.

The Camino is a most sacred of experiences.

Bruce and Lucy

Chapter 4
Day Three

That night, over supper, I chat up my hostess, a gruff and busty woman who serves us pork chops and fresh cheese from her farm. "We might get snow tomorrow," she says.

"Snow!" I look down at my sunburnt arms. "But it was 25 degrees and really sunny today!"

My hostess laughs and pats me on the head. "Ma chère, this is the Gévaudan. Weather here turns like that. You are from Québec, non? You should be used to snow?"

"Well, yes, but not during the summer when we've been having a week of hot weather."

"What can I say? You're approaching l'Aubrac."

I had heard of Aubrac. Aubrac is wild, desolate and hauntingly beautiful. You can get miles of rich evergreen forests followed by empty fields of gray boulders set against deep green plains and scotch broom everywhere. Normally these open plains are heavily populated by grazing cows in the spring and summer only to empty out during the frigid and dark winter months. The openness of the area leaves room for some dangerous times during storms and snowfalls, and you can walk for hours before ever seeing the slightest hint of civilization. Life here would be beautiful and organic, but also lonely and full of solitude.

The French government has offered incentives to get young people to set up an agricultural practice in this region, but to no avail. We walked through private land where rumor had it that 40 years ago four large families had run the farm, making it fruitful and prosperous. Now only two middle-aged male farmers were left, unmarried ("What woman would want to live out here?" said one walker), raising cattle. But as they did only a little gardening, the land was reverting back to its natural state, becoming overgrown by wild plants, moss and trees.

"Whatever is going to become of the farming practices here?" I ask a fellow hiker who had told me that he worked for years with the Aubrac people as part of his food-processing business.

"Ah, that is the question." He shakes his head. "They have traditional practices where the cows wander freely, well-fed, the land well cared for, but no plans for it to survive over the next generation! There is no money for the young ones, they all leave for the city."

"Isn't the government taking notice?"

"The government! Bah! The government tried to set up a green farming initiative that would attract universities and such. The people voted against it! They like this way of life."

I liked the Aubrac way of life too. It was raw, simple but hard, and I imagined myself buying a stone cottage up on a hill and writing by the fireside. Of course, this was honeymoon tourism talking. We heard many stories of the bitter loneliness of the shepherds and farmhands, the lack of money and resources for the farms. Despite the beauty of the land and their pride in raising cattle in full contrast to mega-farming corporate practices, there was also doubt that not enough residents would be left in fifty years to take care of the land. Houses and acres of gardens already sell for next to nothing.

Having the Chemin de Compostelle go through Aubrac was therefore an extra source of income for most farms. They would open up a bed and breakfast and the money would pay for their children's tuition at school and university. The cows were their livelihood, the pilgrims their cash.

We set out on our first day into Aubrac with reservations at an inn 32 kilometres, or 20 miles away. "Oh non," said Marius our Swiss friend, "this is too far."

Some pilgrims undertake the walk for purposes of solitude and therefore walk alone, finding people to commune with in the evenings and on the odd bits and pieces of the trail. Others undertake the trek for purposes of community and therefore set out with companions, finding moments of solitude here and there along the way. Then there are those who are not particularly interested in solitude but have neither brought companions along with them and so create their own Camino community, talking to everyone, walking with anyone at every turn and corner.

This, I had found out, was Marius' case. I still couldn't get over the fact that by the time we started at Le Puy, he had already walked for 35 days. The man had seemingly found Nirvana somewhere in the Swiss Alpine forest and was now doing the rest of the Camino for kicks. There was never a cross word, a sarcastic comment, a frown upon his face. He would stand at the top of the path waving us forward, "Oé! Bonjour le Québec!"

He was also mastering the art of journaling. The second night, when he saw me pull out my journal and mark in the date, he was gleeful at the idea that someone else was keeping records of the trail. "What are you writing down?" he asked me.

"Well, what we saw today, who we met …"

"Here's what I write," he says, rubbing his hands together, "I start with our place of departure and the town we arrived in. The hour I left, the hour I arrived. How much time I spent walking. Then, the number of steps I took that day, I have a pedometer after all, and the number of accumulated steps I have take since leaving Geneva. I also jot down the number of kilometers I walked during the day, and the cumulative kilometers I have taken since the beginning, and the name of our inn. Then I begin actually writing."

"Clearly," comments Nic, "you are doing nothing to dismantle the stereotype of the Swiss being a somewhat calculating people."

Calculating or not, Marius was the reference for all things Camino-concerned. What to eat for lunch: "You must eat in a balanced fashion. Bread, dried sausages, sardines, avocados and some apples. Mmm, j'adore!" When to take a rest: "Every hour, take off the bag, rest for five minutes. It is essential."

And as for the 20-mile day, he was immoveable. "I have made reservations at an inn nine miles from here. Stay there with me tonight. Here, take my phone." But we politely declined thinking, "All right, it will be difficult, but we can make it."

Ego, pure ego.

The snow did not come. But the rain most certainly did. Not one hour after we left, the rain began to fall, and it wasn't light. It was heavy, and wet and cold. It might as well have been snow. People took out every possible layer of clothing they had and wrapped themselves in it. I began developing a routine. Stop, drink something warm if there was a cafe or a farm, change your socks, care for the blisters, hoist the bag, walk on.

In the afternoon we left the group at our lunch spot (a barn with picnic tables where the hostess served full hot lunches) and ventured in the pouring rain towards the woods, a long two-hour stretch of dense forest. We were all alone. Being alone is the worst for the inexperienced walker. It is terrible when you're cold. The physical pain is one thing. But once your mind begins drifting into wishful thinking ("a hot bath, a warm fire, a dry bed") or worse in to de-motivated thinking ("I really hate this. I am in so much pain. When can we stop? I wish we could call a taxi.") then the walk becomes intolerable and every step a challenge. Stopping can be fatal because you think you will never have the strength to get up again. Our last three and a half miles that day nearly did me in.

Three and a half.

By the time we arrived near the end of France, three and half miles
would go by in a blink. It would be the length of one long conversation,
one simple stretch of road. It would be so easy I could swear that I
could fall asleep while walking three and a half miles. But on day three,
three and half would take over two hours and be a struggle from
beginning to end.

"Where is the stupid house?" I cried. "Come on, Jen," was all Nicolas
could reply. He was at his end too, his face drooping, his back bent, his
feet sore. We walked more in silence. The kicker for me came when I
had to pee. By the end of the day I had to pee a lot—this may have
been from my level of fatigue. I wandered into the woods and tried to
pee through my urine cup. I must have been holding it wrong because
the next thing I knew, my pants were all wet. "Are you kidding me?" I
muttered. "I've got blisters that are open and sore, muscles that can no
longer move, every square inch of my body is wet and now I have pee
all over my underwear? What the *AARG!!*"

"Everything OK?" Nic called to me.

"Uh huh!" There are some things you just don't tell your mate, out of
concern for the sanctity of your marriage. You let him read about it,
some time later, while he's editing your memoir.

We walked for what felt like forever and the rain stopped, but dark gray
clouds brooded over us. And then, out of the blue, we saw at the end of
the village a long road leading up the farm gate. We'd arrived.

I was so excited, I could have peed my pants.

That is, if I hadn't already done so.

I have heard of hospitality referred to as a gift. The gift of hospitality.
As if to say that someone was particularly blessed with a natural talent
of hosting strangers in their homes, eating at their tables and sleeping
in their beds. In the Bible, there are stories of hospitality linked with
divine intervention. For example, the prophet Elijah is the guest of a
starving widow and her son. "Shall I feed you and then die myself?" she
desperately asks him.

"Give me flour and oil," he answers, "and your flour pot shall never empty and your oil jar shall never run dry." And so she feeds him for a year and his prophesy comes true. Eventually he brings her ill son back to life. She saved his life through her willingness to feed and house him, and in return he gives life back to her.

Or take the story of Rahab, the innkeeper and prostitute of Jericho who risks her life to hide two spies from Joshua's army. In return, they save her life and that of her family's.

The portrait of hospitality in these narratives is so much grittier than the Martha Stewart floral place-setting image we give this word nowadays. Hospitality could literally be a question of life or death, a service that was life-saving and life-giving. It was a deeply spiritual act, divinely ordained, dangerous and in many cases, involving the blind faith of a woman. In Western upper middle-class circles, a good hostess can be almost a parody of the stereotypical house and home of the 1950s. But we would do well to remember that in certain eras and even in some present-day societies, a simple act of welcome could have a lasting impact on someone's life.

In the tradition of the Camino, we were told that hospitality along the road was a considered in Medieval times to be as big a part of the pilgrimage as the walking itself. It was a way for peasants, farmers, invalids, landowners and women to participate in the pilgrimage without doing the walk, which would be difficult for many people who had responsibilities at home. In other words, by being a good host, you were a pilgrim yourself, as much as the pilgrim you were hosting.

In 65 days, we stayed in 65 different places. My head never hit the same pillow two nights in a row. We met hosts who were in the hospitality service for financial reasons. They were business-savvy, or income-hungry. Then we met those families who were passionate about hosting. You could see the level of professionalism in what they did. Typically they served the fanciest meals and had the nicest linens. They could run a five-star hotel and no doubt do it well. And then we stayed in places where the hosts were hospitable by vocation. These were the ones that did not necessarily have the prettiest rooms or the finest meals. But you left there feeling that they had taken care of you physically, emotionally and spiritually. These were the ones who took an interest in who you were and made sure you were going to be able to walk one more day. They gave you peace and silence if you were exhausted, chatted with you if you were feeling friendly, lent you a listening ear and a word of comfort if you were discouraged. And how they discerned what to give and when, I know not.

We arrived at the end of our third day of walking and I quickly calculated we'd been walking for nearly ten hours, in the rain and cold. I felt tears. That night, I would cry myself to sleep out of sheer exhaustion. A stout man in rubber boots was waiting at the barn door.

"Bonjour," says Nicolas.

"Les québecois?" asks the man.

"Yes, that's us."

"Ah," says the man, seemingly relieved, "we've been waiting for you. I asked everyone who came in if they'd seen you, and no one had! Come in, come in."

In no time at all he had our shoes stuffed with paper, our clothes hanging by a fire, our beds assigned, and I was shown where to take a hot shower.

"I do apologize. The place is a bit cramped tonight. Normally we have ten, but tonight, 14. We didn't want to turn anyone away in this weather." We shook our heads. No need to apologize.

"I'm sorry. Normally my wife would talk more. She's exhausted," says Nicolas, looking at my glazed expression.

"Non non non, do not worry. Do not apologize. Look, here comes the wife with the food!"

The food. His large-boned, jolly wife—this couple were just too fitting for an organic milk farm—pulled out a tuna-tomato quiche. Then a plate of smoked sausage and pickles. Then a veal and vegetable stew. Then a cheese plate, straight from the farm. Then some bread. Then some wine. Then some custard pie for desert.

"Bon appétit!" They declared cheerily.

You see? Hospitable by vocation.

The next morning, the air was crisp and the sun was bright. My clothes were dry, my body rested. My foot, bandaged, disinfected, taped and carefully slid into my shoe. I was ready to hit the road.

Chapter 5
Aligot

Now a few days in, I have come to the conclusion that visiting France is as much a culinary trip as it is a pilgrimage. The French pride for local cuisine and produce is obvious: Vegetables straight from the garden, fresh meats, cheeses made right on the farm, pastry desserts cooked to perfection. Most housing along the French trail works off the same formula, the demi-pension. The demi-pension includes your room, supper and breakfast for one set price. Most villages where we stopped for the night have limited accommodations and even fewer restaurants, so you really have no choice—you eat and sleep under the same roof. Not that given the choice you'd go anywhere else. The hosts normally prepare a feast for their guests. The ambiance of the trail is very much created around the meal times at night. Everyone eats together; and when you eat together, you laugh together, you talk together and then the next day you even walk a bit together. Never underestimate the ability of wine and a four-course meal to weave the bonds of community.

Especially if aligot is being served.

Aligot is the hiker's elixir. Picture this: You've been walking for six hours in a rather cool climate, with strong winds, lots of sun and altitudes high enough that you are somewhat weather-beaten by the time you arrive at your destination. Your body is cold, hungry and tired.

You take your shower, lie down for a bit and warm up. Then you go downstairs to the common area which has a large hearth and fireplace, stone walls, long wooden tables and benches. You are still tired and aching. Then the aligot meal comes-- mashed potatoes with cream, butter, garlic and tome--a wet, stringy cheese--and the whole thing makes the potatoes cheesy and gooey and thick and so freakin' delicious you want to cry.

The first time I tried aligot was on day four. Day four was especially good. Mostly because it wasn't day three. After the nightmare of day three, day four was a walk in the park. Actually, it was a walk through Aubrac, with its gorgeous plains and incredible wildflowers, tiny chapels and the beginnings of stone garden walls. I can't particularly remember all I saw that day. But I can remember that all that I saw was particularly beautiful. And windy. My face was definitely weather-beaten by the time I got to the inn, a sweet little country cottage-type with a flower garden and a surly innkeeper.

I stood at our balcony, and to my pleasure, welcomed all the walkers by name. Only four days in, and I knew all these people by name. That was amazing for a trip during which most of the time spent walking is spent alone. We all sat down in the evening for the meal and the cook walked in with a huge cauldron and a large wooden flat spoon. I sat next to Kit and Jane, and we gave each other blister updates as the cook started stringing the aligot out of the pot. He lifted the spoon several feet above the cauldron and the mixture hung down from it. Twist, twist, twist and plop! Down on to the plate.

"Oooh," said Kit as she spooned her first helping. "I never want to eat anything else. "

I tasted the aligot, and nearly swooned. "Where has this been all my life?"

Warmth spread through my body and nothing, not a quilt, not a shiatsu massage, not even a bubble bath would have felt as good.

Fresh tome really is the magic ingredient. This cheese is made throughout the region of Auvergne, and more specifically in this sub-region of Aubrac, which is south-central France, and used primarily for the making of the scrumptious aligot. I've read up as much as I can on tome fraîche and some sources claim that the monks developed it specifically for the pilgrims on their way to Santiago di Compostella so they would receive a hearty and nutritious dish to give them the strength to walk the next day.

You walked and then you needed aligot. Now the opposite can be said: you eat aligot, then you need to walk. The mashed potatoes are actually a "modern" rendition of aligot. In Medieval times, they served it with cut up chunks of bread, more like a stew.

Tome fraîche possesses three essential attributes. It must be cow's milk, it must be raw (i.e., unpasteurized), and it must have a very short aging period. That last one is the catch. The French directory of cheeses states that the maximum maturation period for tome should be ten days. The tome we ate in Aubrac had only matured for three days. Coming back home and searching for the perfect cheese was an adventure in itself. For Quebec cheeses, the youngest tome I found had an aging period of 30 days. I went from cheese shop to cheese shop asking for "tome fraîche" and would consistently be offered "tome de savoie" which is a firm, yellowed cheese which really doesn't accomplish the same stringy effect.

Then, one day as I was surfing the Internet for solutions, chef superstar Ricardo's web site popped up. He had just done a show on aligot. Beautiful man! Big smiles and all, he explained that you can use young cheddar. Of course! We may not have tome, but, by God, do we ever have cheddar. The trick therefore is not actually having tome (of course, die-hards from Aubrac are cursing my name right about now) but to have a young cheese, because this is what creates the stringy, silky texture of the dish. We are lucky in Montreal to have a cheese shop that carries fresh-of-the-day cheddar, imported from the farm every morning. It resembles, both in taste and touch, a block of cheese curds. It's quite moist, chewy and it sort of squeaks and melts in your mouth.

Once you've figured out the cheese dilemma, you're home free. The aligot basically makes itself. I won't bore you with the details of its fabrication...well, if you insist.

Ingredients:

Aligot

4-5 large russet potatoes

4 garlic cloves (more if you like a very garlicky taste)

1/2 cup crème fraîche

1/4 cup butter

1/2 cup whole milk (or enough for potatoes to have a nice creamy texture)

1 cup of young cheddar, fresh of the day preferably

Salt and pepper to taste

Directions:

Boil a large pot of water and peel the potatoes. Cook them well in boiling water, so that they break easily. Using a strainer, steam the garlic over boiling water until it is quite tender.

Drain cooked potatoes and transfer to a mixing bowl. Add butter and milk. Begin beating so that they have a smooth, creamy texture of mashed potatoes. Add the garlic and make sure it is well blended into the mix.

Add crème fraîche, and salt and pepper to taste.

Cut up cheddar into small slices.

Return mashed potato mix to the stove top over medium heat. Add in cheddar slices and with a large wooden spoon, begin to stir in large, generous gestures. Be sure to not let the potatoes stick to the bottom of the pot. Once mixture is bubbly and it begins to string, like long elastics, as you lift the spoon, it's ready.

Just how good is this dish? I mailed my sister a postcard with the recipe for aligot and she tweeted us a week later: "Have made and eaten the aligot. Now want to live in a vat of aligot for the rest of my life."

Chapter 6
The Backpack

There is perhaps no topic of conversation more popular around the dinner table than that of the weight of your bag. The unwritten rule of female etiquette which states that others should never know what is in your purse has been completely thrown out the window. Not only do a dozen of my fellow walkers know the contents of my carrier, they have analyzed them in depth over a glass of wine at supper time.

"Well, let's see, I have one sleeping bag ..."

"How heavy? What's the stuffing?"

"... two pairs of underwear ..."

"Only two? Hmm, good for you, maybe I need to get rid of one. What's the brand of your undies? How much did they cost?"

"... Two pairs of merino socks ..."

"O non, non, non, that will never do. You don't wear wool on the Camino!"

And so on and so forth. Then comes the elimination process. On the first night, my new friend Célia actually had a road companion come into her room, empty the contents of her backpack and throw out anything that said road companion deemed superfluous, just to have an objective point of view.

"Did it work?" I asked

"Oh yes, she really went crazy. Threw out a second bra, a skirt, a salt shaker..."

"You brought a salt shaker?"

"I like my tomatoes with salt. Tastes very nice. But those grams really were weighing me down ..."

Célia's not the only one who went to town on her bag. We heard Camino legends of people sawing the arms off their toothbrushes, tearing out a page of their guidebooks once they were done with the info, snipping off the strings of their bags...anything to gain an ounce here or there.

Then, of course, once you're done purging and feng-shuing your bag, you need to estimate if it passes the body-weight ratio test. Ten per cent, they say, of your entire body weight. Which means that itsy-bitsy skinny Célia's 26-pound backpack was far too big, while heavyset, Alpine Swiss Marius's 35 pounds passed the test.

I never weighed mine. I just put it on when it felt OK.

Now when I say "put it on," I should probably clarify: One does not just put on the bag. One hoists, bounces, and adjusts the bag for probably a full minute before one begins walking. Getting the bag ready in the morning goes something like this:

Roll up sleeping bag, put in first. Heavy stuff on the bottom. Assemble medicine kit after finding random items strewn here and there around the room. Ignore husband's complaints concerning my disorganization. Put in med kit, clothes, hairbrush, journal. Take out hairbrush, get hair into ponytail mode, put hairbrush back in bag. Ignore husband glaring at me from outside the window. Roll up raincoat, put it on the top (easy reach in case it rains), put blister pack in top pocket. Ignore husband's groans and comments about how we may get to Santiago by Christmas if we're lucky. Hoist bag on back. Tighten straps, clip bottom, clip top, pull strings, pull strap. Zip coat. Clip, clip, string, strap, zip. Grab walking sticks. Let husband know we are on a peaceful Camino in which one practices patience and compassion and maybe Mr. Efficiency-obsessed should take advantage of our pilgrimage to acquire some of these virtues, because, after all, we are all here to better ourselves. Start walking.

Damn. Forgot the water bottles. Hold on a minute. Gotta go back.

The Backpack: The Husband Speaks:

The thing about backpacks is that you can have all the rules in the world, but it really all comes down to whether or not you can walk comfortably with the weight on your back. That's what I told the wife, anyways, when I saw her putting her entire knitting collection into the bottom of her pack, and then run over to the body-backpack-weight percentile calculator on the computer. "Carry it for an hour and see how you feel," I said, and in an unprecedented gesture of actually listening to any counsel I've ever given, she did. And then dumped her knitting collection.

The walking is the first thing I think about in the morning, and the last thing I think about at night. I crave the air in the morning, especially when it's early, especially when it's quiet. Truth be told, I've never worked harder, but I've never felt lighter. When the bulk of the walking gets done before the brightest hours of the day, say, around 3 p.m., that's when I feel the best. The sun isn't beating too hard, the road isn't too noisy, you have time to explore your rest points and destinations, you have time to unwind at the end of the day. The morning is when you're energized, and if you're energized, the backpack isn't too heavy. So walking early on in the day, it's not just about timing, it's about enjoying the road.

I got teased by some Camino friends the other day about my overly timed routine, but really I don't have a routine at all: Just, do bag. Grab poles. Hit the road.

That sums up this morning. I pack my belongings, which were folded next to the bed from the night before, I stuff them in my sleeping bag, I lace up my shoes and walk outside where my poles are hanging on a hook. That's it.

The Backpack

Ready to go. The road looks beautiful, the air is fresh, some fellow pilgrims pass me at the gate waving goodbye. Turn around. Can't find the wife. Go back to the room.

Wife is getting out of the shower. "Be there in a sec, honey!"

Dump bag. Dump poles. Shuffle off to the dining room for second coffee.

Chapter 7
A Woman's Right to Pee

Dedicated to Christa Smith who was going through a hard time and needed a good reason to smile.

Historically, the pilgrimage to Santiago di Compostella was a man's route, navigated by kings, dukes, monks. and priests, rarely to be journeyed by women. There are many factors for this: Pilgrimages were physically arduous, even dangerous. The roads were haunted by wolves, thieves and other such riff-raff, and therefore inappropriate for the female class who needed to stay home and tend to the farm whilst their male counterparts were busy winning their spot in paradise.

Of course, one could also guess that women didn't walk the Camino because there were simply not enough rest areas along the way for them to stop and pee, but this could be a chicken -and-egg phenomenon: Are there not enough toilets because women entered the pilgrimage context too late in the game, or did women become pilgrims much later on, and therefore there are no toilets? In any case, my problem with the Camino is crystal clear. While the Catholic dioceses of Europe and the numerous pilgrim associations have diligently placed chapels, churches (which, by the way, are categorically toilet-less—did priests in the Middle Ages never have to go?), water pumps, markers and picnic tables along the road, there is a sad lack of bathrooms.

There are solutions, of course. Before I left, our regional pilgrims' association, Québec à Compostelle, told me to buy the Whiz-Easy, referred to by Nicolas as the "Super Lady Cup," which looks like a purple (oooh, purple for girls!) funnel with a spout. The package says that this eco-friendly, hygienic, comfortable tool has been tested "by 1,400 women from different walks of life, all who attest to its fun and practical nature." Well, you 1,400 women from different walks of life, I hope your sense of coordination is better than mine, because the Whiz-Easy was quickly renamed the Whiz-Impossible, and eventually became the Whiz-oh-forget-it-I-give-up! It was then promptly disposed of (who needs the extra weight in one's bag? Not me) after a few unfortunate incidents involving the infamous gadget, a shady area, a full bladder and some very wet underwear. My search for ideal peeing circumstances continued on.

I developed what I call the "inner pee-dialogue." It went something like this:

Walk, walk, walk, Hmmm, I have to pee.

Walk, walk, look at the cows Hey, there's some sheep. I really have to pee. When's the next village?

Walk, walk, quieting my mind, breathe deep, look at the sky. OK, now it's bad.

Walk, walk, such beautiful scenery. Oh, sod it, I need to PEE NOW.

Find a tree off the path. Nope, not that one, too exposed, need a better shaded area. Tell Nic to wait. Look around, make sure no one is near. Move deeper into shaded area, pray none of these plants are poisonous. Take off bag ... clip, clip, strap, strap. Unzip rain coat, pull down pants, pee. Awkward fumbling around for Kleenex, then the eternal debate with what to do with the Kleenex - throw it on the ground and hope for rain so it disintegrates? Keep it with me and hope for a garbage can, which can be rare and sometimes nonexistent? Never sure.

And on it goes.

Enter Jane and Kit, the mother-daughter team of American walkers who dealt so deftly with my blisters in the first days. At first I was fooled by their sing-song voices and the cutesy names, but I have come to see that these two are tough cookies who have a faster pace than just about anyone on the road, despite sore tendons and bad knees. I love that Jane works for the Peace Corps in Lebanon, and composes songs about our mishaps on the road. And Kit is just plain one of the easiest people to talk to in the whole bunch of us walking this particular stretch of road. She continually checks in on Lucy and Bruce, ever since she treated them, and jokes about the threading and draining without so much as a pursed lip. This alone would be enough for me to be naturally drawn to these two. But then they also say hilarious things, such as, "Oh sure, you can get over the blisters, but then what do you do about the diarrhea?!?" This creates such a sharp contrast to all the French prissiness around me ("That meal was inadmissible!") that I like them even more.

We commiserate together about the toilet situation—you have to keep drinking because dehydration brings on a slew of fantastic conditions such as fainting, tendon rupture, stomach cramps, muscle strain, vomiting, and other such lovelies. You also need your caffeine in the morning because if you don't drink coffee you won't get walking fast enough. (I have given up TV, my bed, my privacy, my shoes and generally looking cute. But not my coffee.) So you're going to have to pee. It's going to happen.

"OK, hon," says Jane to me one morning after gulping down the rest of her coffee, "catch ya later in the bushes."

A couple of hours later I am walking and the pee-dialogue begins again. Is there a village coming up? Can I wait 15 minutes? Oh look, a nice church ... a nice church without a toilet. Darn.

This is all going on in my head when suddenly I hear behind me, "Here we come!" And I turn to see Jane and Kit sauntering up the path, only to climb up to an ever-so-slightly shaded area, squat down, drop their pants and begin to pee, backpacks on, bums exposed in front of God and everybody. I am stunned, but my path is clear.

"Wait for me!" I call to my new gurus, and I climb up behind them to follow in their footsteps. Then, just as I am about to grab some tissue, I watch in astonishment as—marvelous women!—they hoist up their trousers without the merest hint of a Kleenex, not producing a single square of toilet paper. I follow suit. I am wearing $30 fast drying underwear after all. Let's put these babies to work. I watch as Kit and Jane scamper off, relieved and satisfied. I smile. These are my people. This is where I belong.

Chapter 8
The Price of Beauty

When I was a child, I read *The Little Mermaid* by Hans Christian Anderson. In the tale, the Little Mermaid strikes a bargain with the Sea Witch to exchange her fins for legs in order to be closer to her beloved human prince. The Sea Witch gives the Little Mermaid her legs, but takes her voice. Also, she tells her that every step she takes will be excruciatingly painful, like someone driving a knife through her chest, every time she walked. And then the Sea Witch tells her she could never go back into the ocean, never ever again.

At the time, I remember thinking that the whole thing sounded like a fate worse than death. Why would the Little Mermaid be so willing to live with such pain simply to be near the prince, who had not even returned her love? This made no sense.

On day five we walked from Aumont-Aubrac to St-Chely. We walked through mountain plateaus of lush green meadows sprinkled with white narcissus. Tiny abandoned stone houses and shelters which shepherds now use to make cheese were nestled on the top of hills, set against a clear blue sky. Cows grazed the pastures cut through by low stonewalls making the landscape look like a quilt of green tones. It was a beauty, a stabbing beauty that caught your breath and made you gasp.

The Price of Beauty

I was walking on blisters, Lucy and Bruce were far from healed, and every step I took caused me to wince. Only five days in, and my feet were suffering. My toes were squeezed and pinched between the bandages. The blisters were wailing. Nothing was yet healed. And all of a sudden, it didn't matter. I would have gone for days like this, if it meant I could continue walking in this scenery.

What is the price of beauty? What are you willing to pay to have your heart struck by the view surrounding you? People will build a house on the ocean and pay thousands of dollars to install a bay window for the view. But expensive real estate is not the same thing as the beauty of a discovery of Creation, so surprising, so overwhelming that perhaps only the suffering to attain it can truly measure its cost. Perhaps only through the hurt of ugliness and of pain can one really understand and appreciate the worth of beauty.

The Little Mermaid was willing to pay for love with the daily suffering caused by pain. I realized that day that I was willing to endure searing blisters and limping in order to gain proximity to the beautiful. The price didn't bother me that much.

Shortly after I decided this, my feet stopped hurting.

Chapter 9
The Middle-Aged Man

We are heading out of St-Chely, around day six, when we see Kit at the bank. "Hi, Kit!" I call out. "Still off the foot?" She nods, putting on a pout. "Ankle's still swollen", she sighs. Two days ago, the blister on her toe caused her to walk in an odd manner for too long. She had shifted the weight onto a bad place on her foot, causing an injury to her ankle. Just one of the many casualties of the road, but unfortunately for her, she and her mother were on a time limit and so couldn't afford to stop and recover. Jane walked the stretches and Kit took a taxi and waited for us at the next village. Her Camino would come to an end pretty soon, much to my dismay. "No walking today. Where were you guys staying last night?"

"At a gorgeous inn right up the road," I replied. "Unfortunately, we were in the room with Eduardo."

Kit gasps. "You know, my mom has a crush on him."

"Well, tell her to cut it out. He'd make a terrible bed partner."

"That bad?"

"The stuff of legends."

She gives us a sympathetic smile. "Well, with any luck you guys'll get your own room tonight."

"With any luck we won't even be in the same town as Eduardo."

Poor Eduardo. He was absolutely the sweetest Italian man I'd ever met. Great dinner company. Buys his fellow pilgrims wine every chance he gets. Tells good jokes. Unfortunately the affection ends there. The man snored so loudly you had to hold onto your bedstand for fear of being vacuumed in through his nostrils. So bothersome was he that the word on the road was that if you walked into an inn and saw him sitting at the table, there was but one thing to do: promptly turn on your heels and knock at the local parish church's door, begging for mercy, in the hopes that some kind-mannered monk would offer you a cot on the floor. Anything but sleeping in the room with Eduardo whose snorts, whistles, wheezes, sighs, coughs, groans and snores were sure to keep you wide awake with stress and frustration into the wee hours of the morning.

It's not just Eduardo, though. The Camino is chockfull of middle-aged men traveling alone, disturbing people's nights with their maladjusted uvulas, obstructed nasal passageways and sleep apnea-related breathing handicaps. Don't get me wrong. I have endless admiration for the middle-aged male pilgrim, those tall sturdy types showing the beginnings of silver hair and bulging middles. These 50 plus-ers were often the image-incarnate of the road—worn and wiry. I hardly met one of them who did not exude kindness, happy to be out in the fresh air and away from the office, especially affectionate with the younger pilgrims because we reminded them of their grown children. They came in the tens of dozens, most of them retirees or almost retirees, searching perhaps to ground themselves in something authentic and organic after a career at a company that they maybe no longer believed in, living a life whose material comforts perhaps no longer made them happy. The Camino, in many ways, is an alternative to the mid-life crisis. I'm good with that. I'll take a friendly, contemplative hiker any day over a man who cheats on his wife with a woman half his age and drives a convertible. Fine by me. Speaking of the wife, it was often remarked upon that there very few middle-aged men who came with theirs. People speculated that wives of that age were often no longer fit enough to walk alongside their husbands. Or maybe she wasn't retired yet. Or maybe the kids, albeit teenagers by now, still needed one parent at home. I have another idea. She may just have jumped at the opportunity of having three weeks of uninterrupted, blissful, quiet sleep, what with the hubster gone away in search of himself. Here's the scene:

"Chérie, wouldn't you like to come with me?"

"Non, non, mon amour, you need some time for yourself ... I'll stay with the kids."

"But they're away at university!"

"Oh is that so? Hadn't noticed ..."

"You've always said you'd like to see the Pyrenees ..."

"Yes, dear, but I'd also like to see the season finale of *So You Think You can Dance.*"

And the whole time she's thinking, "The bed to myself, the bed to myself ..."

It may not seem like such a big issue, but take my word for it, this is not slight nighttime noise, this is a well-tuned esophagus emitting snorts, scrapes and honks of gurgling thick mucus-filled snores. Now, I know that my 30-year-old husband will one day too be a loud, groaning, humming snorer, but we're not there yet and I don't plan on being there for another 20 years. When that day comes I will do what all the other wives haven't done: Drop my husband off at a sleep clinic and tell the specialists to work their magic. In any case, I too will be 50 by then and no doubt menopausal, graying and flatulent and so it'll all be fair game.

I am also aware of the sacrifice made by these men to be on the pilgrimage. They are rejecting society's prescription for happiness in search of something bigger than themselves. They are leaving behind house and home in exchange for sore muscles, fatigue and loneliness. I appreciate that. But really, middle-aged men, this one's for you: Man up. Swallow your pride, put aside the taboos and ego and admit you have a problem. Or if you didn't know, listen to those who are revealing new truths about your nocturnal behavior. And buy some nose strips.

The Middle-Aged Man

Chapter 10
The Camino Question

We meet Albert a few days in on the road. Albert has kind eyes, and slightly graying hair which gives him a softer face than most. Everyone meets up one night in Espalion, on the eighth day of our trek. "So," he says to Nic over supper as he lights up a cigarette, "Newlyweds?" "No," Nic replies. "We'll be celebrating six years in Spain." "Well!" replies Albert merrily, "Then you two don't need to sit next to each other at the table!" Everybody chuckles.

Albert tells us he did the Camino last year, but missed the stretch from Le Puy to Conques. "Unfinished business," he says matter-of-factly. "Oui, mes amis," he speaks to all at the table. "Le chemin is like one long year of therapy. This is how it works: You set out by asking yourself a question. The road takes care of the rest."

I feel Jane nodding beside me. "You agree?" I ask her. She shrugs. "Well, hon, I've been living in Lebanon for three years, you know, with the Peace Corps. But my mom is 92 years old. My son's about to have a baby. It's time to go home. I guess I didn't need the Camino to tell me that. But sometimes you just need to think a little and make sure your decision is clear. What about you?" she asks Yan, our Dutch friend.

He coughs a little nervously. I get the impression that opening up to total strangers is a little counter-cultural. "I quit my job three weeks ago. Couldn't take the sales world anymore. The pressure to perform, you know? So, I thought, I need to walk for a while and figure out what I want. I think I truly put too much on myself, though. So maybe I was the problem all along and not the job." He exhales as if this revelation was strangling him. Total strangers we may be, but apparently this place is the one for raw and total honesty.

OK, so everyone has a question. "Do you have a question?" I ask Nicolas the next day as we climb over a hill. He shrugs, "All I know is, you can't do this trip without some underlying, spiritual motivation. It's not tourism, that's for sure."

"I don't think everyone's here for religious or even primarily spiritual reasons."

"I mean they have a question in the largest sense." Nic pauses, "You know, bettering oneself, finding out what's important in life, that sort of thing. Being willing to undergo pain and suffer the discipline of forcing yourself to walk every day, just to do the work of the Camino."

"It is sort of work, isn't it?"

"Definitely more work than taking a trip to Paris."

"But do you have a question, you know like Albert was saying?"

"Not sure."

"Me neither."

"What's the deal with Albert?" asks Nic.

"What do you mean?"

"How can a non-retiree afford to go not once on the chemin but twice within the space of a single year?" he ponders.

"I was wondering about that You know he's got two kids at home?"

"How old?"

"Eight and ten. I asked him last night whether he missed his family and he sort of shrugged. Then he said he'd be lying if he said yes. You mark my words," I turn to Nic and drop my bag, ready for a rest. "I bet his question has something to do with his marriage."

We were sitting at a cafe a few days later when Albert comes to join us. Nicolas offers him a beer. "This trip is finishing up for you soon, isn't it?"

"Sad but true," replies Albert. "Tell me," he asks, "How's your marriage taking the chemin?"

I look at Nic a little bashfully because just that morning I'd railed on him that he was still walking too fast and would he mind taking consideration of his wife once in a while and accept that she's not exactly like him and furthermore this does not mean she's inferior to him. Actually, I said a quite few more things. Nic takes my hand and winks at me. "Never better," he declares to Albert. Wonderful man!

"I've seen marriages split up on the Camino, is all. For all sorts of reasons. One partner feels they were dragged into it against their will, another one decides they need a change and the spouse doesn't agree ... or then there's the classic reason."

"What's that?" I ask Albert.

"They spend all this endless time together only to find out that they can't stand each other's company."

"Oh," I say, feeling all of a sudden sad but relieved. "Well, we like each other's company a whole lot. And this was something we'd been planning since forever. We'd talked about the pilgrimage even before we were married. It really was our common project."

"Best case scenario," Albert responds.

"Our problem is we still need to work on accepting each other."

"What do you mean?"

"Our rhythms drive each other nuts," cuts in Nicolas. "I like to plan my day a certain way, Jenna has a far different way of doing things. She takes more time in the mornings, she talks longer at the breakfast table, she wants more breaks on the road, she's less careful with money ..."

"He means I worry less about money," I interrupt, shooting Nic a look. "I just want to bask a little more in each experience, Nicolas would like a little more time-efficiency."

Albert looks at us going back and forth and throws his head back and laughs. "It's called marriage, kids!"

I turn back to Albert. "Would your wife ever want to do the trail?" I ask out of guilty curiosity.

He sighs. "No, this isn't her thing. In fact, there aren't many things that are her thing. It's been a bad couple of years. First, I took a job that obliged me to live in another town. When that didn't work I transferred back and hated my new position. So I sold my share of the business to my bosses and decided to work from home on my own projects. Then her existential crisis began. The kids are more independent, she has no raison d'être, she's alone, she's bored ... so I say, 'Fine, you're bored. So go and do something, find a hobby, get a job, go back to school.' She does nothing. But is still bored. You know, by transferring back to a job closer to the house I was choosing family over career. It was a bad choice. "

I feel stunned by his last statement. To say that one prefers their career over their family seems like something of a taboo. Or maybe this is only true for women.

"It's hard being a woman," I say softly, wanting to defend this wife I'd never met, just a bit.

He nods. "I know this. But there's a distance between us. Our paths are going in separate directions."

"Is that why you came back to the Camino?"

He nods. I give a subtle look to Nicolas. You see? A woman's intuition. He squeezes my hand. "Does your wife agree?" I ask.

"I'm not sure she sees it as clearly as I do. But she will. She must. Well, mes amis, I promised to dine with Anya and Anneke. Have you met them? Little rays of sunshine ..." And he gives a wave to two Dutch bombshells across the way. "Tally-ho, as they say in Britain."

He tears off.

I look at Nic. "What did I say about his marriage?"

He shakes his head. "Kind of sad, don't you think?"

"I guess. You know, I recognize there's always two sides to every story, and I don't want to discount how miserable it must be to be stuck in a dead-end marriage. But it's a little disconcerting to think of a wife stuck back at home caring for the kids all alone while her husband is traipsing along the road under the guise of spiritual enlightenment while flirting with cute Dutch girls." I nod in Albert's direction, who is now walking towards the restaurant, his arm around Anneke.

"It makes you a little crazy, doesn't it?"

"I don't know ... vulnerable more like."

The fact is, Albert's story was scary. You want your marriage or you partnership to be OK. Actually, you want it to be better than OK. You want it to thrive and be peaceful but exciting, loving yet challenging, but if it can't be all that, you hope that you'll just make it through to another anniversary without wanting to kill each other, or worse, not caring. Albert spoke of his wife as if it didn't matter what she would go through once he announced he wanted out. His purposes and desires were seemingly so much more important than hers. What was really upsetting was that Albert would not be the only person we'd meet on the Camino who told us they wanted out of their marriage. I never knew how to take these poor unfortunate souls. Were they copping out? Truly soul searching? Just simply confused? Or just in search of an affair with some unassuming fellow pilgrim?

I asked Nicolas, months later whether he thought Albert had actually gone ahead with his plan and left his wife and kids or whether he'd tried to fix his broken marriage.

"Neither," was his reply. "People in need of an escape do just that. Escape and never confront. To leave or to fix would have required a fair amount of head-on confrontation. Nope, if you ask me he went back to his cushy house and his unfulfilled wife and has been there ever since, daydreaming about his fantasy life with Anneke."

So much for the Camino question. It's only as good as the action that follows the answer.

Chapter 11
Prayer

I am not forcing myself to pray with words. I'm not sure I much believe in prayer with words anymore. I was raised in a church that had too many words. Prayers would go something like this: "Lord, I pray for my sister Élise who was diagnosed with cancer, stage three, in the left lymph node of her neck. She is being treated by Dr. Charbonneau at Hôpital Sacré Coeur and has her next appointment on Tuesday at 3:15 p.m., Lord. Lord, you know that she is not a follower of your Son Jesus Christ even though she had a conversion when she was eleven and a half in our backyard with our brother Robert and our next door neighbor, Marie. Lord, I just pray for her stage three cancer of the left lymph node in her neck, that you would intercede in a rapid and authoritative manner, that Dr. Charbonneau at the Hôpital Sacré Coeur would be guided by your divine hand and provide the correct treatment for her and that she would, through this experience, be revealed your true nature and that she would turn to you. Lord, at this time I would lift up her son Thomas, who also does not know you. Lord, he is eight and has dyslexia ..."

I spent my childhood prayer times utterly and completely bored. I don't find that evangelical Christians are particularly good pray-ers. They lack the hundreds of years of poetical liturgy that the Catholic, Orthodox and Anglican churches have, they lack the drama and emotion that Judaism has, they definitely lack the silence that the Quakers and

Eastern religions have, and they lack the reverence and respect for sacred spaces that I have found that Islam has in spades. They sound more like business executives listing off their company's needs and assets: "All right, so here we've got strength and stamina, but over in marketing we will need direction and guidance, so that the task may be carried out with diligence and fervor. Meeting adjourned."

By the time I am comfortable in the daily routine of getting up, packing, hitting the road, we are about seven days in. The Camino is relatively quiet these days, according to many experienced pilgrims and hosts. We see people at resting points, but soon lose each other until the end of the day. Nicolas and I spend much of our time alone on the path.

I begin to think about what I want for my mind and my heart. After all, I am accumulating hundreds of hours in nature, in quiet, without the distractions of phones, computers, people, TV or melodramatic teenagers at the youth center where I work. They always would walk into my office, needing right at that moment to tell me about "the worst day of my life."

I should take advantage of this space I have been given. But I refuse to force the prayers. I decided this at the beginning of the trip, and I have kept my promise. Certain churches along the way have little booklets for the pilgrims of meditations, songs, Bible passages. I pick one up, and I like it, but I do not intentionally insert any aspect of the booklet into my daily walking. I have been so trained, so taught, so talked to about the formula upon which we Christians must live our inner and outer lives. There are enough books written about praying that their fibers could replenish the rain forests. My early morning prayer meetings at college were good for me socially and spiritually, but for those of us who wouldn't pray out loud, there were bound to be questions about whether we were "all right with Jesus." Try telling them that you're fine with Jesus, that it's their style you've got more of a problem with. No deal.

Therefore, no more forcing the prayers. Whatever needs to be spoken will be spoken, the rest will come as it is. I won't force it, but I will create space and time for it. I will trust that God will take care of my praying, if I need to pray.

I do however begin to say the Lord's Prayer. Once in French, once in English, to make it last a bit longer. Not necessarily because I think that God needs to hear it, or because I need to fill the silence. On the contrary, I want the silence to remain as such so that I hear God filling it. But I begin saying the Lord's Prayer to center myself, focus in on the fact that I am praying. If I don't say it, my mind tends to drift in and out of my meditating on God. The meditative aspect of my walking becomes choppy, cut up. So I say the Lord's Prayer and during those words my mind is focused nowhere else but on the space between myself and God, on the calm that I am seeking from Him, on the reverence that I am feeling in my prayer time.

Still, I don't force the Lord's Prayer either.

Some mornings, it's the first thing I do. As soon as we are out of town and onto the path, I speak it, silently, in my mind. Some mornings, I say it around 10 a,m,, when we've been walking for a bit because we started out with other walkers. Some mornings, I don't feel I have the mental space for it, so I wait.

One morning, on day nine, an interesting thing happened. We had quite an ascent into the town of Estaing—probably 300 yards up in a very short space of time. Estaing is a beautiful town, built on a river called the Lot, which you cross over on a very old stone bridge. A large fifteenth-century castle overlooks Estaing, built into the mountain range. A sign with the Templar cross greets us at the top of our climb, indicating that Estaing has been a popular resting spot for pilgrims for many centuries. And you need a rest after that morning's climb. Everyone was sweaty and out of breath. When you hike like that you're not thinking of much else. Just one foot forward, then the other foot forward.

I reached the top, panting and breathing so heavily. I let out one giant sigh. As I did, "Our Father, who art in heaven," the first line of the Lord's Prayer, simply slipped off my tongue. My heart still pounding, my breath still heavy, I was caught off guard by the words simply coming out on their own. The rest of the prayer came out as easily. The prayer had engraved itself into my breath. After that I knew I wouldn't need to think about it anymore. It would come if it needed to. Barely a

83

Prayer

morning went by for the rest of the Camino that I didn't utter its words.

Chapter 12
Conques

Twelve days in, we have arrived in Conques, or as the Americans call it, "Conk." Conques is the resting place of Sainte-Foy (Saint Faith), a martyred 13-year-old in the year 303. It seems to be the mission of the people of Conques to preserve this town as it was on the day of Saint Faith's death.

A village of stone houses set against a stunning backdrop of thick green forested mountains, Conques' narrow cobblestone streets descend on tight angles, so that most cars never even access them (motorists usually park at the top of the town and walk in), leaving it all open for pilgrims, residents, donkeys, chickens and bicycles to wander freely through the twists and turns among the pale yellow buildings. Every single building is adorned with rose bushes of complementary shades of pink that climb their way over ancient wooden doorways. There is not one square inch of Conques' infrastructure or façade that could be called ugly. It's no wonder that this tiny hamlet, population 281, was named a "Grand Site" of France and is an appointed member of the "Plus beaux villages de la France" (the Most Beautiful Villages in France) association. There is a collective concern for aesthetics in Conques, every stone in its rightful spot, every window beautifully dressed. Nothing seems out of place, but neither does it seem contrived.

Truly, this town is a living, breathing relic of history. The only problem is that it knows this, rendering Conques both a UNESCO gem and a tourist trap. Thankfully, the numerous postcard stands, pottery stores and Medieval accessory shops kind of meld into the background (no doubt because of strict municipal laws on signage and storefront aesthetics, for example, no neon billboards) and do not take away from Conques' charm.

Nicolas and I had spent a rather hot day of walking through some serious forest elevations. So stepping into Conques is like entering Rivendale, but instead of sexy female elves, there are monks. We don't walk 50 feet before Nic asks me if we should stay an extra day.

"After all," he says, "we've been walking for over a week and we haven't taken a break since we began."

"Let's stay," I reply without hesitation.

We aren't the only ones who want to settle down for a while here. We walk into a craft store where the British salesgirl tells us that she too was walking the chemin until she happened upon Conques. "I just stayed," she says matter-of-factly.

"You just stayed? Never went back home?"

"Well, I mean, I closed up my life back in London, but yeah, I set down my bags and never looked back. It was time for a change."

All right, then.

The heart of the town is without a doubt its abbey. The abbey is run by a community of five monks who pretty much run the show, acting as tour guides, hosts, spiritual counselors, liturgists, gardeners, school teachers, musicians, merchants and cultural curators. They're also quite a friendly bunch. On our way to breakfast, one monk stood at the entrance of the kitchen waving us by in his white cloak singing, "Vive le Québec!"

We stay at the abbey on the first night, an experience that confirms the now seemingly international truth that Christian organizations are big on heart, low on efficiency. There are approximately twelve volunteers who greet us at the bottom of the steps, top of the steps, entrance, hallway, courtyard, shoe rack and drink table, all giving us the same rehearsed instructions ("Welcome! Boots on the rack, poles on the hooks, please have some punch and registration is to the left ... Welcome! Boots on the rack, poles on the hooks, please have some punch ...") and asking us the same questions: "Name please? Do you have a reservation?" Despite the overwhelming amount of chit chat, they all seemed to possess the same utter lack of pertinent information, such as what room we are in.

Once we get through check-in, which is apparently an unavoidably long process due to confusion over reservations, faulty billing, and a lost key to the room, a very kind and very enthusiastic elderly volunteer, Jean-Pierre, leads us up a dark stone staircase, built in 1100. "I would point out at this time," says Jean-Pierre solemnly, "that you are not the first pilgrims to have climbed these stairs."

After we walk through the library, we arrive at our room which overlooks a beautiful Medieval courtyard. Jean-Pierre then proceeds to tell us in great detail the schedule of the Masses, Vespers and morning prayers, giving elaborate descriptions of each service, giving no attention to the fact that we are actually holding a printed schedule in our hands. He wishes us a good stay, reminds us a third time that vespers are at 6:30 p.m., and promptly leaves us before we have a chance to ask where the bathrooms are, whether there is a washing machine in the vicinity, or what time supper is served. With all due respect to vespers, these were the things we were really concerned about.

However, I may have been wrong that the only really important things were laundry and meals. Even if they didn't realize it, the monastery volunteers had it right all along. The meal actually doesn't matter. Laundry? What laundry? You can do laundry anytime. The Vespers, though ... the vespers.

Here's what happens when you go to Vespers. You drag your tired, aching, hungry body over to the sanctuary. The benches are a little hard, the stone floor a little cold. No matter. Everyone around you looks as weary as you feel. The man across the aisle has a bandage on his foot, the woman next to him is massaging her knee. Your neighbor is examining a blister. The tourists are told to hush or get out and the lights dim. There is still some evening sun coming in through the stained-glass windows. We are quiet. There is so much quiet around us, except for some faint sounds from children playing outside. Then the monks sing. Everything is candles, and readings and quiet. Most of us in the sanctuary are walkers, and the priest knows this. So he talks to us and reads Scripture in four different languages. Then he prays for our safety and wellbeing. This isn't just a feel-good moment. This isn't just an Enya song, or a pretty piece of scenery. As the priest speaks and prays, you know that you are participating in something sacred, something more different than anything you've ever done in your life before. It's not just Mass. It's not just another service. You are receiving a blessing. I find it significant that in this tradition, the congregants' prayers are actually carried out by the prayers of the priest. During the Reformation, Protestantism reclaimed the right of the individual to pray, confess and access God without the priest acting as intercessor or messenger.

While I understand the theological value of this, I am grateful for the Catholic tradition in which I am participating at this moment. The priest prays for us, in our place. I am tired. My presence on the bench and my silence are all I can offer up at this moment. The priest knows this; he is taking our walking, our presence, our fatigue, and he is contributing his words. Don't speak, he is saying to us. Just rest. I'll do the speaking for you. This is why the liturgy is a blessing. It accepts and affirms that, sometimes, we don't have the words. So it puts the words out for you. And you know that you are now part of a tradition, a practice, a movement. And the priest knows this, too, murmuring through his prayers what we are feeling every day, in and out, step by step.

Then we are quiet again. And you think, through your sore, aching muscles, that maybe you've never felt so good.

The Vespers. The Vespers.

Following the service, we step out for a pint and find our "512 Division." Albert christened us the "512 Division" because we'd all left Le Puy on the 12th of May. We've counted about 20 people who left at the same time. We meet each other in zigzag fashion, either at a cafe along the road, or a day later at the same inn where we all dine together.

I make a habit of sitting at a table in the main rooms of the inns and say hello to our people as they wander by. I remember their names. Nic has a harder time. This is a great complementarity between us. I know people's names, he reads maps so we don't get lost. The 512 Division are my comfort blanket in those first few days on an unknown trail. Nicolas and I are not ready to be hermitic monks, despite of our love of quiet, and I look forward to meeting up with various members of the 512 so that we can compare war wounds, hiking stories and developments in our respective "ditching of equipment."

"What have you thrown away today?"

"I mailed back a jacket, a purse, three pairs of socks and two guide books."

"Ouch! I'm not even sure I brought that much to begin with!"

"What can I say, I'm a person of caution."

We met Yan at our fourth-day stop. He's sharing a room with us. I like him. By the time we had walked a few days with him, both Nic and I had developed a fond attachment for Yan, our new Dutch friend, looking forward to seeing him at every stop along the road and meeting up with him at the end of every day, as he awaits us with a beer in hand. I haven't met many Dutchmen whom I couldn't get along with. Stocky, tall and soft in demeanor, Yan talks with us with ease and candor. He also walks at the speed of lightning, inheriting the nickname "the flying Dutchman" from some fellow pilgrims. No matter how early Nicolas and I leave, the usual tradition is to arrive at a stop along the way and see Yan sitting on the terrace of a café, sipping his morning latte. In the afternoon, it'll be a Heineken or a glass of wine.

"How do you do it?" asks Nic. "We left an hour before you did this morning and here you are, waiting for us at the next village."

Yan laughs and says, "Actually, when I told my wife I was the fastest walker she was not too pleased with me. You see, I am a little bit of a workaholic at home. This is why I decided to do the Camino."

"You push yourself too hard at work?" I ask, feeling strong empathy.

He nods. "I've been thinking about it, you know, the Camino question and all. People tell me I'm far too hard on myself. So my wife wanted me to learn to slow down."

"Yan," I say, raising my glass, "it's like looking in a mirror. That is, if I were 45, male, Dutch and about four feet taller. But really, a mirror."

"And you?" he asks us, "Why did you decide to do Compostelle?" There's that WHY question again. I let Nic answer, for I never really know how to sum it up. I never think to ask that question myself. It's a state of being. It is what it is. I see our 512 friends doing the walk and I suppose, if I think about it, they're all seeking something from the road. But the Why has become less important for me than What I am actually experiencing. I say this to Yan.

"The What right now is the absence of materialism."

"I agree with you. When I left my job the first thing my son asked was what was to become of the company car we had."

I laughed. "He's a teen."

"I know, but you have to ask yourself, is this how he's going to be? What have I created?"

What have I created? I think that might have been a driving question for the 512 Division, albeit not in those exact words. Most of our members were pre- or new retirees, baby boomers, middle classers who were reflecting on or reacting against their lives. Disillusioned by the companies they had worked for, the lifestyles they'd bought into, and sorely sad about the materialistic upbringing they'd given their children.

I talked about this with my French friend, Célia. Célia had been retired for just two months before undertaking Compostelle. "Oh, là!" she gasped. "Do you know what my job was? I was in charge of logistics for the transport company that imported children's goods from China. Do you know the level of stress I endured day in, day out for all those years? If we were late by so much as five hours for delivery, we'd receive a huge fine. So I would stay at the office until all hours of the night, phoning trucks, distributers, border controllers. I lacked sleep for that job, I missed family suppers for that job. And for what? Garbage that children will throw out after two months of use! It's so meaningless!"

Robert, another 512-er concurred. "In the seventies, we were all in love with the ideals of our companies. Even in the private sector, you offered a service. A good product that would better the lives of the general public. That's what it was about. Then the Reagan era hit, and everything was about the bottom line. 'You can make a profit off anything,' we were told. That bottom line nearly killed me. My company sacrificed some of its core values for that bottom line, our integrity for that bottom line. And then came the children ..."

"What do you mean?" I asked.

"We were told to give you everything," piped in Célia. "Our generation didn't have as much, so we didn't want to deprive you of anything."

"I lived under the impression that if I didn't buy all the ski lessons, the gifts, the school trips, the clothes, that not only was I a bad provider for my family, but that I was somehow hindering my child's education."

Robert sighed. "My kids are not as autonomous as I would like them to be now. I think I must have given them too much."

Célia pats him on the hand. "We all fell under that spell, dear. Not just you."

Marius surprises us the most. "Aaah," he says in his usual jolly tone. "The work world is so dog-eat-dog. You wonder if it's all worth it."

"Where did you work?" I ask.

"In the banking district." Of course. He's Swiss.

"I was the director of the southwest division of the Swiss national bank," he adds.

Nic and I freeze. "Good God," Nic whispers to me. "We've been sitting at the same table talking about bleeding toenails and athlete's foot with the principal shareholder of Switzerland!"

Marius shakes his head, "No ... it was so much. Too much, really. It took me away from life."

I listen to these outpourings with interest but distance. These are realities that are completely different from my own, and yet our worlds are intertwined. I've complained many an hour with my university pals about how our parents and grandparents built up the American Dream, ruined the planet, fed a corrupted economic system. And here I am, talking with those who were right in the middle of it and they're as weary as I am. They're tired out from the image they've been slaves to, turned off by the consumerism and sick of the lies of the work world.

I look at them and see the victims of a Western culture. They have no answers. Only emotions. I've never spent such an extended period of time with people who are in a whole other generation than my own. I love the intergenerational aspect of this group. We are the youngest by far, Nicolas and I, adopting the name, "les petits québecois" or "les petits canadiens" depending on how each individual feels about Quebec's sovereignty debate. They all assume that because we are young, we must be poor and so they consistently pay for our drinks at the table, a favor we insist on repaying in Conques.

Conques is a bittersweet reunion of the 512s. On our day off, we have the chance to see every last person. We grab a table in the center square, in front of the monastery and one by one, our original group trickles in, each one being greeted with an uproarious, "Hey!" by all of us seated. We sit in a large circle, like the cool crowd at the cafeteria, staring down the loser tourists who will be driving to the next towns, not like us tough cookies who've been walking for twelve days already.

We know that after Conques, the 512 Division will be splitting up. We said a somewhat tearful goodbye to Kit and Jane who had to head back to Paris in order to catch their flight. I thought remorsefully how much fun it would have been to walk the whole way with them, whining about our blisters and spotting the road for each other when the other person had to pee. Not to mention the good conversations. But it wasn't meant to be. Jane needed to get back home to her mother, and Kit's injured foot wouldn't hold up much longer.

Little by little, each person's Camino will be finishing, and only four of us will be going on to Spain. We sit around exchanging email addresses like kids on the last day of summer camp. I feel a tug at my heart as Marius tells us that he will be taking it much slower, seeing as his hip has been acting up, and the chances of us seeing him in a week will be quite slim. We thank him for all the good advice. I am touched when Chantal, an experienced French hiker, cries as she says goodbye to Nicolas and me, calling us her "rays of sunshine." I pay for Albert's beer and think about how much I will miss his animated fervor for conversation.

I am worlds apart from most of these people, both in generation, financial status and life story, but I experienced a connection to them that I am grateful for. I bask in that last pub run with the 512 Division, truly enjoying the company of these misfits, these 50 plus-ers who of their own accord have left professions they no longer believe in, a world of financial materialism and ecological irresponsibility, in the hopes of finding something more important. I look around the table and wonder, and hope that they have found it, if only in part, on the French chemin de Compostelle.

Conques

Chapter 13
Maryse

Since the abbey only gives out beds to those who have walked into the village that day, we need to find lodgings for our second night in Conques. Nic makes a few calls to some places in our book, and we get a spot at Chez Maryse. He makes the reservation and shakes his head.

"I hope it's OK. I had a really hard time understanding her, and she definitely had a hard time understanding me."

"Because of your accent?"

"I think it had more to do with her hearing."

"Do you at least have an address?" He shakes his head.

"Nic!"

"Jen, this town is a ten-minute walk from end to end. How hard could it be to find this place?"

We walk into a pizza parlour and ask the woman behind the counter if she knows Maryse. She gives us a smile. "Maryse is La mère du village -- the mother of Conques. Of course, I know her. Are you staying with her tonight?" I nod. "Well, you're in luck. It is a most fantastical experience."

I look at her quizzically. "You'll see," she says, and scribbles an address on a piece of paper before disappearing into the back.

We wobble up a windy cobblestone path and arrive in front of a very dark door, having to tip our heads a bit to the left in order to see it clearly. I look into the courtyard, and see a bowl of cherries on a chair with a sign that reads "3 Euros—for the patients at the hospital." A slightly hunchbacked woman answers the door and gives us a toothy smile. "Mes pélerins!" My pilgrims!

Jean-Daniel, the head monk of Conques is standing behind her and gives us a large wave. "Ah, oui! These fine walkers were with us last night. They come from Quebec, you know."

"What brings you over here?" asks Nic.

Jean-Daniel lifts a basket of lilies. "Maryse provides the flowers for the sanctuary. And did you notice the cherries? She sells those for our patients at the psychiatric hospital. And she sells honey for the school."

"So she pretty much runs the town."

"Ha-ha!" Jean-Daniel laughs. "Pretty much."

"Come, come." Maryse ushers us in. We walk into her house and I have to lean on an angled banister to see it straight. I am guessing the house was built around the 1700s, at a period when 90-degree angles and solid foundational structures were not a priority. There is literally not a straight beam, floor, stair or doorway to be found in the whole place. We walk into the guest room.

"Wow," comments Nicolas, "This is like being in one of those optical illusion rooms at the science museum. Are you feeling a bit woozy?" I giggle as I throw my sweater on a chair, missing. It's a bit difficult to gauge distances in this room.

We hear a knock at the door. Célia enters in. "Mes amis, do you have a plug-in here? I need to charge my phone." We motion her to the wall behind the bed. She sticks the charger in and immediately all the lights in the house go out. "Good grief!" exclaims Célia. "What in heaven's name happened?"

"Ah, non!" we hear Maryse cry as she scuttles towards us, gibbering about a whole lot of things I can scarcely understand. "Frappe! Frappe!" I gawk at her and then realize she is telling us to hit the wall. Célia, Nicolas and I look at each other, puzzled. Maryse grunts in exasperation and grabs a broom. Thwack! She hits the wall, and the lights immediately turn back on.

"Well," says Nic. "We know the structure of this house hasn't been touched since about 1805. Do you suppose the fuse box predates or postdates that period?"

Maryse, understanding no English, turns to Célia, oblivious that the scene could possibly have caused any commotion. "Ma chère, I know your room is on the third floor and it can be a hassle to traipse all the way down in the middle of the night to relieve yourself. Here you are." And with that, thrusts a chamber pot into Célia's stunned grasp, and promptly saunters off, leaving us in hysterics.

Maryse

Chapter 14
Moissac

The road to Moissac is long and hard. Literally. Mile upon mile of black asphalt which scorches the soles of your feet. It took nearly 19 days, but we have finally hit the dreaded "ugly stretches" of the French road. Yan has a theory that your physical pain and your boredom only really hit when you don't have anything pretty to look at. Today, that theory proved to be true. We see Yan near the end of the day. He was putting his cell phone away. "My wife has asked me if I have had much of chance to sort of think through my questions about the future. I said not really. So she told me I could keep walking to Santiago if I wanted."

I laughed. "Does that mean she's enjoying her time without you?"

Yan laughed back. "That's what I asked her!"

Yan had a point, though. None of us were really thinking intentionally about our "Camino question." Most of us agreed that during the day, your mind just drifts in and out of reality. You don't analyze, you don't decide anything. You just are. Some people swear that they have fallen asleep while walking and only wake up an hour or two later. I feel this is not so much a state of sleep for me as an emptying of my mind.

Today, what with the scenery not being so great—all that asphalt— my mind was taken up by thoughts. I allowed different things to come to my attention. Instead of trying to distract myself from all that could stress me out—a memory from home, a situation with a kid from work, a worry about the center—I decided to let myself think about it, but not dwell on it, and then gently, organically, I could feel my mind move on to something else. All of a sudden I would realize that I wasn't focusing anymore on the kid, the job, the worry. My mind had moved on. Today, there was a consistent flow of clips and excerpts from movies, TV shows, CDs and concerts we'd been to recently. It's like my brain was detoxing itself of years of useless sounds and images, purging thoughts, worries, stresses that just didn't need to be there anymore. Actually, they never needed to be there in the first place.

In Moissac we stay at the Ancien Carmel, an old Carmelite monastery set up for pilgrims. It is now run by a volunteer association of big-hearted, well-meaning, disorganized lovers of the Camino, who lose our reservations and accept full responsibility for their disorganization, fluttering about in order to find us a new room.

One of the volunteers, Martine, tells us that she was a full -blown atheist before doing the Chemin de Compostelle. "I am not a believer any more than I was before, she said to us. "But I did the Camino last year and I feel grateful towards religion. Religion made the road. And the road helped me. So now I volunteer at the Ancien Carmel."

I talked about this with Nicolas later on. "The Ancien Carmel is an historic Christian organization. Funny how Martine, who's a self-proclaimed atheist would volunteer there, don't you think?"

"The thing is, Jen," replies Nic, "we Catholics don't think like the Protestants. You don't need to come to faith first and then put it into practice. You participate in the works, in the practice and your faith follows. The works lead you into your journey of faith. They don't need for the individual to come gift-wrapped as a believer. They just need them to come. The theology says that we must trust that once they come, they'll believe."

"So a total pagan could go be a missionary in Africa or something?"

"Well first of all, how many 'total pagans' do you know who would actually sign up for a mission trip to Africa, and second of all, yes, they could. What do you think this pilgrimage is actually about for a lot of people? Sure, you meet devout Catholics along the road, but you meet a butt-load more of people who don't have a clue what they believe. The road is open to them anyways. You're allowed to do the work of the road, to participate in its experience. It's a gift that the Church offers to anyone who wants it, regardless of lifestyle or belief. Do the work, God will engrave your faith."

"Tell that to all the people who get absolutely nothing out of the pilgrimage."

"Let us proclaim the mystery of faith," Sings Nicolas mockingly.

"I'm serious! What if it doesn't work?"

"So it doesn't work. All I'm saying is that evangelicals have it wrong. You guys make someone sign a confession of faith and take a six-week course on baptism so that they can go chop onions in some church-run soup kitchen. And then you point fingers and say that evil Catholics believe you can—oh my!—be saved by good works. Tell me something: When was the last time that evil came out of someone's good works?"

I wince. "They just say that you can't only have works and not faith."

"And Catholics don't disagree. They just say that the works can be your vessel towards faith. Give it a little push. And that faith is difficult, mysterious, whereas the works ... well, when your faith is faltering, or in crisis mode, or in Martine's case non-existent, you can always fall back on the works to help you move towards belief. It's a method of participation. Shouldn't atheists be allowed to participate in the kingdom of God? Shouldn't they be allowed to walk the road to Santiago, even if their own reasons have nothing to do with the Church?"

Moissac

Chapter 15
Charles

We are about three weeks in when we enter the County of the Gers, which is located in the Midi-Pyrénées region, meaning quite far to the southwest. The Gers stand in the shadow of the Pyrenees, boasting neither its population, majestic mountainous landscape or economic strongholds, but they hold their own. Fields of wheat and sunflowers not yet in bloom, orchards upon orchards of fruit trees, vineyards, cherry and apricot trees, rivers and valleys, the Gers suited me just fine. The people are extremely proud, not only of their history—this is the region of the Three Musketeers—but of their alcohol.

First, you have the Armagnac. Armagnac's slogan is "the oldest alcohol in France". Its distillation process was developed by the Romans over 700 years ago. Distilled from white wine, it holds a minimum content of 40 percent alcohol. Its grapes are carefully selected from certain vineyards in certain areas of southwestern France and housed in oak barrels. It's sweet, thick and fairly dangerous for those of us who have a low tolerance to alcohol. Of course, for the average southwestern Frenchman, a full cup of consumption seems to be the daily average after which they no doubt shove back their chairs and continue working the tractor. Everything is relative.

Then you have the wines in the family of the Côtes de Gascogne. Many of them are white, but you can find red and rosé as well. The wines are good, but nothing in comparison to the notorious, celebrated Floc de Gascogne.

Floc de Gascogne is a fruity, summery, after-dinner drink made up of watered-down Armagnac and unfermented grapes. Only 17 percent alcohol, it's a walk in the park compared to the Armagnac. Still, an evening of supporting the local economy through its wine produce can be quite an adventure. Especially if your body is tired and slightly dehydrated.

We arrived in Lectoure near the end of May. Lectoure is another one of those Medieval cities built in a teardrop shape, somewhat elevated and totally surrounded by forest as a means of defense. Lectoure, like many other towns and regions, navigates in a modern world on the infrastructural backdrop of the old one. The town's population is no more than 3,000 people, yet they've witnessed, firsthand, nearly every event that shaped France's history. The only exception is the Second World War, as it belonged to territory that was unoccupied by Nazi Germany. This sets the Gers apart.

Their bridges, churches, roads and walls were not bombed by the weapons of modern warfare, while neighboring countries, not one day's drive from the houses in the village, were crushed to smithereens. They have therefore developed, I feel, a cultural psyche that is anchored in pride and preservation.

This is one of the things I appreciated in France. Joni Mitchell's lyric "you don't know what you've got till it's gone" doesn't apply here. To be sure, the French are infamous complainers, whining about everything from train schedules to globalization, but as far as history, culture and beauty are concerned, they know they've got the corner office on those. And so they promote it.

Lectoure falls into this category. They promote their local economy and history, their wines and lifestyles. While researching this town, I fell upon the City Hall website, and what do I find? A municipal program dedicated entirely to recruiting, relocating and integrating urban independent workers into the countryside of Lectoure. "You work by telecommunications?" reads the advertisement. "Then come live in Lectoure." And then there's this very seductive picture of a pretty mother, toddler by her side, working on a graphic arts project on her laptop, sitting on the grass in a vineyard. I tell you. And this is in a country where only eight percent of the population works by long distance, comparatively low to the rest of the world.

But that's the message of Lectoure: "We know we're so great that we are investing money and time in getting urbanites not to just visit, oh no, that's for amateurs, no, they're going to LIVE here." As an urbanite, I can see the appeal. The escape from the city and its massive concrete towers towards a small countryside town, with buildings that do not exceed four stories and streets are all only one or two lanes wide. The urban life can seem uselessly busy and large in comparison. Or so Lectoure would have the urbanite tourists believe, anyways.

In Lectoure, we stayed at Marie and Charles's house. As we step onto their back porch, Marie immediately dotes on us, bringing water, juice and beer. Charles walks out. "Ahh, nos pélerins!" rubbing his hands together in a devious fashion. Upon hearing we're from Montreal, his face breaks out into a smile. "I lived in Montréal in 1957 as a student! I was a boarder in the Plateau with a very old woman."

"You wouldn't recognize the Plateau anymore. It's changed quite a bit. Gotten fancy. Gentrified."

"Well, it wasn't too bad where I lived. Corner of Sherbrooke and de Lorimier."

Nic and I glance at each other. "Say what, now?" I ask. "Not exactly on the corner of Sherbrooke and de Lorimier? In a three-storey stone building?"

"Yes, that's the one," Said Charles. Nic and I burst out laughing.

"That's where I lived as a student," I say, amazed. "2105 Sherbrooke."

Charles smiles, pleased with himself. "Well, there you go. We lived in the same building. You see?" He turns to his wife. "This is what the chemin is all about." And then he wanders off, showing no more signs of surprise at the fact that two people from different walks of life, more than 40 years apart and thousands of miles between them, would wind up at the same dinner table, only to find out they had been neighbors, give or take 60 years. Like this sort of thing was to be expected. And maybe it was, given Charles's story. More about that later.

"I liked Spain more than France," he says without reserve. "France is for the tourists. Spain is for the pilgrims. I started out a tourist, you see. In my life, I was an atheist, even an anti-clerical," he adds, lowering his voice, as if the real travesty was not his disbelief but his disdain of organized religion. "But on the Camino ... well ..." His voice gets soft, and he looks away. "Well, that changed. And so you see, Spain was no disappointment. No, Spain was the pilgrimage."

We sit down for supper and Charles pours us all a French portion of Armagnac. I should define "French portion." In the simplest of terms, the wife takes out a generic glass the size of which can play host to apple juice, water, wine or, in this case, a drink laced with 40 percent alcohol. The content matters not. Only the container does. And the container is almost always full. Nic and I stare into our glasses, silently calculating the time-food-alcohol intake ratios necessary in order to avoid him getting too philosophical and me climbing up onto the tables and singing "O Suzanna."

Marie serves a feast—breaded veal, homemade soup, pasta with melted cheese. I ravenously scarf down the carbs as Charles talks to us.

He was born in Spain, he tells us, to parents who were blacklisted under Franco's regime. His father and mother were finally imprisoned when Charles was three years old. At the time, when mothers were prisoners, they had to take their children with them. No child protection laws back then. So Charles, from the age of three to five years old, lived in a prison cell with his mother and 10 other women and their children no bigger than his kitchen (about 20 square feet).

Under Franco, according to Charles, the nuns were in cahoots with the authorities. It was all the sisters from the local monastery who ran the prison, "and they beat the children when we cried," shaking his head. "Finally, my priest, the one who baptized me, stepped forward and told the police that they could not in good conscious continue detaining a child in those conditions. I was comatose by the time they pulled me out." He was malnourished, beaten and underdeveloped, but was at long last released along with his mother, on the condition that they would leave the country, which they gladly did and wound up in France.

"I've been French ever since."

"So you lived the best and the worst of the Church," I said. "The nuns nearly killed you and the priest saved your life."

"Hmm," replies Charles. And then pours us more wine.

He then proceeds to tell us about the first time he did the Camino, taking the Puy-en-Velay road, same as us. "It was the beginning of April, you see, and so I had packed both summer and winter clothing." He was two days into l'Aubrac and having the sunniest of sunny weather, he says, "22, 23 degrees Celsius ... so I began ditching my winter clothing!" He had a winter hiking jacket that got sent back home, along with some polar underwear, a sweater, some merino socks and a thick pair of pants. He kept his shorts, windbreaker and tee shirts.

"Classic pilgrim mistake," Charles says, shaking his head. "Getting rid of too much equipment in order to save weight, and assuming that the weather in Aubrac would be the same as in the rest of France." The weather in Aubrac has been known to turn on a dime. Once you're in an elevated part (usually in the forest) you can have a drastically different weather pattern than in a lower part of the region, be it a mere four or five miles behind or ahead of you.

This is precisely what happened to Charles. "I entered the woods," he shrugs, "and all of a sudden, I was in the middle of a blizzard. That very same morning, my road was set against a clear spring sky. But by afternoon, the winds had really picked up."

Having a difficult time calculating exactly where he was, and consequently not knowing if it would be better to turn back or keep on going, he decided to keep going. The problem was, with the thick woods and the blizzard clouds, it didn't take long before he couldn't see two feet in front of him. The snow was really coming down hard and his vision was completely impaired. "And the whole time, wearing nothing more than my hiking shorts and a windbreaker!" he laughs.

Charles

I turn to Marie. "And you had no idea your husband was on death's door at this time?"

She smiles. "Oh no, dear. April is a beautiful time of the year in these parts. I was busy cooking supper for our pilgrims that night."

Nic and I shake our heads in awe. "So what happened?"

"Well," he continues, as he tops up our glasses. "I decided that I better not keep on walking. Couldn't see the path—the snow was now up to my knees. So I dug my walking poles into a snow bank, and to keep warm I circled it." Then, when he could no longer feel his digits, he told us he said his last prayers and fell asleep. I could only assume that by this time both his atheism and anticlericalism had been ditched along with his winter wear.

"You really could have died," says Nic. "Isn't falling asleep the one thing you're never, ever supposed to do in the cold?"

Charles shrugs his shoulders again. "I'm not sure. But let me tell you, I couldn't fight it. Just curled up and dozed off."

And then he says he woke up. The snow had stopped. The sun was out.

"It was very, very bright. I think I may have been asleep for no longer than 20 minutes, but it felt like forever." He walked only a bit, and as he turned the path, he saw a farmhouse. Good thing, too, because he was wet, dehydrated and frostbitten. He knocked on the door, hoping for a charitable soul. An elderly woman and her sister opened the door, took one look at him and fell into near hysterics. They ushered him in and didn't let him get a word in edgewise—not that he could have talked had he wanted to. "I was frozen stiff!" They led him to the fireplace, pulled out every thick blanket they could find and then stripped him naked.

I stop eating. "Naked?"

"As the day I was born. What was I to do? They were two, I was one, and not much strength was in me at that time. My faculties were completely compromised … more wine, Nicolas?"

"Ummm ..." Nic hesitates.

"I'll take that as a yes." Wine glass fills up. Charles continues with his story.

"And so I sat, frozen, fatigued and in the nude in front of the fireplace as two hysterical women scurried around me drying my clothes, feeding me brandy and the whole time chiding me for my recklessness. So you see," he concludes, "I made peace with my past on the Camino. Like I said, I used to be an atheist. But then ... I changed my mind."

"The funny thing is," he laughs, "all these years, almost all of my life, I've lived here in Lectoure, yet only later on in life did I want to have anything to do with walking the Camino. And when that day arrived, all I had to do was pack my bag and leave, seeing as my house was on the Way!"

Sometimes, when you want to find God, all you have to do is step out your front door.

"So!" he says cheerily, "It's time for the digestif! Floc d'Armagnac !"

"Jenna," Nicolas whispers to me desperately, "I am so drunk."

"Buck up," I reply. "You'll just have to do one more. We're not driving. And the man has just told us about how he found Jesus. If he says drink, you drink."

Charles

Chapter 16
Camino Miracle

I had an adorable blue raincoat. It was long, down to the knees long, with a fitted hood and ties around the wrist so that the water couldn't seep into the arms.

On Day 24 we were deep in the Gers region, almost on the doorstep of the Pyrenees, which means we would soon be seeing mountains. But this day, it was vineyards. Lots and lots of them. And donkeys, and ponies. I lost my raincoat in this land.

I had been losing a lot of things those days which was puzzling to me. Was I living more freely, less concerned by material goods, or was I just tired? Or worse, was I finally losing my mind? Had the quest for spiritual peace and inner silence ultimately pushed me over the edge? Nicolas would have to bring me back home in a straightjacket.

First, I lost my sandal. I had both sandals clipped to my backpack and one must have gotten unclipped when we were sitting down for lunch. We arrived at our hostess' house and I reached for my flip-flop (it's such a nice thing to take off your shoes and air out your feet) and that's when I realized it. One sandal was gone. My beautiful, black, comfortable flip-flop croc. Missing. The hostess, a large, jolly, middle-aged woman lent me a slipper which I positively swam in. Nicolas and I went back and forth on whether or not we should go into town immediately to buy a new pair, or should I wait it out until we get to Saint-Jean Pied de Port, which is a week away. I was humming and hawing over this decision when in walked Célia and Robert. We had arranged to stay at the same inn, as we would often lose sight of each other on the road during the day.

"Look what I found," declared Célia proudly, waving a black sandal at me.

My jaw dropped. "My flip-flop!"

"We saw the Croc insignia and knew it must be Jenna's—it's Canadian, after all! Just lying on the side of a vineyard." I jumped up from my chair and nearly knocked Célia over with a hug.

It's what you could call a Camino miracle. Camino miracles tend to be the smaller things that make your walk just that much more livable. Finding your exact prescription of sunglasses, for instance, at a tiny hole-in-the-wall pharmacy in some lost village. Desperately needing a post office and walking into one that's open. (In France, that's not really a Camino miracle. That's just a miracle.) Losing a sandal along the road and having a pilgrim friend pick it up a few hours later. Camino miracle! I love this newfound definition of miracle. Nothing needs to be big or magical or awesome. In the end, it's the daily little graces that help you pass the time with a bit more joy and peace that are truly miraculous.

We'd had absolutely stunning weather these past weeks—sunny, warm, barely a drop of rain since that infamous Day Three. "Le malheur de l'un fait le bonheur de l'autre," the French idiom states. One's misfortune is another's luck. We were in France during a terrible drought while the European economy was going to shambles. The farmers were devastated, the tourist industry suffered, but the walkers got sunny days and loads of available accommodations. Life could not have been better.

We sat down one afternoon in a cherry orchard—there are loads of cherries around these parts. We had cherry jam for breakfast, cherries for dessert, cherries for snacks. Nicolas declared he would not eat one more cherry ever again for as long as he shall live. "Don't say that," I replied. "They need the sales to boost the economy."

And then I felt a fat raindrop on my arm. I was about to whine, but then I remembered the dozens of conversations over the past few days with hosts, be they farmers, gardeners or friends of either group and how badly they needed the water, so I kept my mouth shut. I opened the top of my bag, where the raincoat was always to be found, and reached down to feel ... nothing.

"Crap."

"What?" asked Nicolas absentmindedly.

"My raincoat is gone."

"Oh, Jen, you cannot be serious."

Quickly my mind swung back a few days to a guesthouse where I had hung my coat in a closet. "We've had such awesome weather these days, I hardly take notice of my rain gear anymore. I left it in the big closet in Nogaro. Dang."

"Jenna!" Nic raised his arms.

"I know, I know!"

"No, but seriously, where are you gonna find another raincoat? Look at where we are!"

He had a point. These tiny clusters of houses gave a new meaning to the word hamlet. All residents of these parts possess a minimum of two cars per household because if you want a doctor, groceries, newspaper, gardening tools or so much as a band-aid, you better be ready to drive for it. Bakeries from nearby towns would deliver their morning baguettes door to door, as do butchers and fruit peddlers. All this to say, a corner store is a rare commodity, and something as specific as hiking gear seemed to be but a dream.

I shrugged my shoulders and looked at my husband pitifully. He rolled his eyes. "You are so scatterbrained, I'm telling you one day something really bad is going to happen."

"Stop!" I sighed.

We walked through Béarn landscape, which was absolutely beautiful. Houses in the Basque style with rusted red shutters and roofs aligned the road, and the greens of the hills stretched out before us. The light rain actually accentuated the colors, and it was warm, so my lack of a raincoat didn't bother me too much. Once we got into Arthez-de-Béarn the sky was really clouded over. "I've got to get a raincoat," I wailed. Weather predictions for the next day were bleak. Our innkeeper pointed me in the direction of town towards an agricultural store.

"I love farmers," I said to Nic as I lifted up a rubber raincoat from a corner shelf. Nic took it into his hands.

"You are not serious. This thing weighs a ton." We kept on digging and I found a lightweight windbreaker-raincoat of sorts that was obviously intended for a burly Basque farmer but that would have to do for a petite-sized pilgrim.

"Camino miracle!" I declared. "What were the chances of finding a raincoat in these parts?"

"You must have a horseshoe up your butt." said Nic, holding my hand. "I honestly thought we were going to dress you in a garbage bag with holes for your arms."

The next day, however, the miracle seemed a bit far away. We took off early in the morning knowing we'd have more than 20 miles to do with Gilles and Jean, a Parisian and a Quebecois whom we'd met the previous day. Célia and Robert were one town away, having decided to cut up this last week in shorter increments, so Nicolas and I were in need of some walking buddies. We'd decided to walk the four of us together because the road was tricky—lots of ways to get lost—and there were terrible predictions for the weather. Why would these be good reasons to walk in numbers? It can only be explained by the famous rule of solidarity: misery loves company.

We were only 20 minutes on the trail before the rain started down in such torrential sheets that I thought I surely would not see 10 meters in front of me. Gilles, a faster walker than the rest of us, turned around with a huge smile on his face, water dripping down from his hat over his cheeks. I giggled at the sight of him. I picked up the pace, trying my best to keep up but it was to no avail. Winds were blowing against us, rain slamming down on the pavement and it took all my strength to not burst into tears. On top of it all, we were soon walking along the side of a highway, with huge trucks whizzing by. "This is hell," I muttered under my breath.

Gilles pulled out his guidebook, attempting to protect the pages from getting too wet. He pointed west. "This way." We all turned a corner and wound up in a tire yard. Yes, a tire yard.

"Oh. My. God." I said to Nic.

"Gilles, are you sure?" he called. Jean shook his head.

Gilles sighed and rubbed his head. "This can't be right." He pulled out an IPhone. "Desperate times call for desperate measures." He marked in the coordinates to the GPS app and said, "OK, Apple, lead the way."

"Remind me to French kiss Steve Jobs next time I see him," I said as we turned in the opposite direction and found a trail marker—the famous Compostelle seashell.

The miracle raincoat turned out to be less than a miracle. It would have worked better had there been no rain—mind you, this was no light drizzle. Our group took a break after five miles of walking, confident we were now on the right trail. We huddled under the wood roof of a shelter and Nicolas removed his shoes, and wrung out his socks. "Oh, là!" exclaimed Jean. It seemed every single one of us had some sort of problem with our equipment that day. The coats, the shoes, the socks, the bag straps. The wind and rain were just getting the better of us, every step of the way.

Finally I simply surrendered. "Fine! Get me wet!" and the icy cold water trickled down my arm to my arm pit. My hair stood on end and I could feel my back turn to goose bumps. I stood up straighter, because hunching over wasn't keeping me dry and I laughed as the rain soaked me right through to my pores. I gave in, stopped fighting it and continued walking—slosh, slosh, slosh.

Lunchtime seemed to never arrive. Pilgrims trudged through to a monastery that had just opened a café for lunch stops. Chapels and monasteries along the Way not only contributed culture and heritage to the walk, but held an incredibly utilitarian function. They were places where you cooled down, warmed up, took refuge from the rain, treated injuries. They were the constant stopping point for walkers. I appreciate to no end this primary function that these old, stone chapels had taken on. In this case, the little annex to the monastery, set to be turned into a restaurant in a month's time, was opened exceptionally early for the pilgrims because of the rain. We were a parade of ponchos and plastic covers, hovering around a fire in hopes of warming up a bit. "Well," Gilles said to us, "it's right around here that you should be able to get the first glimpse of the Pyrenees."

We all guffawed. There was so much rain and fog that we would be lucky if we could get a glimpse of the turns in the road.

The kicker came after lunch. As a result of a change of water and PMS, and six straight days of eating duck (French food is good, but not particularly diversified), I had suffered a three-day bout of constipation. The term "pilgrim's progress" came to mind, because, well, there wasn't any in my case. I had bought some dried apricots in the hopes of remedying my case. The apricots—how could I put this?—they worked a little too well. About two hours after we'd left the monastery, I began suffering some of the worst digestive cramps that I had ever experienced. Thankfully, the guys had walked on, so I sauntered into a cornfield, hopefully out of sight, and relieved myself of four days worth of waste. Nicolas came out to find me.

"You OK?"

"Well, in the words of Bill Bryson, I'm a real man now. I've shit in the woods."

"There you go, I knew you had it in you."

"I had a little too much in me, in fact. Will you ever want to have sex with me again?"

"Remains to be seen."

We finally, finally, arrived at our destination. Navarrenx. Gilles, Jean, Nicolas and I looked at each other like war buddies who had just survived an invasion.

"Friends," said Nic, "I couldn't think of a more enjoyable company to be happily miserable with."

"I concur," said Gilles a little feebly. He took off his shoes and showed us his feet. They were pasty white.

I gasped. "Good grief, Gilles, it looks like you've spent a week in the trenches."

He giggled and said he was actually more concerned about his book, showing us a sopping wet, well-ruined pile of pages. "It didn't fare as well as the rest of us! Come on, I see an outdoors store."

We walked into a small boutique where the owner was apparently going to pay for his kids' braces with the day's profits. Pilgrims lined up at the cash register holding ponchos, towels, new socks and leg guards, all items they no doubt wished they had had throughout the wretched day. I bought bright blue gaiters that made me look like Rainbow Bright. They were designed to hug my legs and clip over my shoes so that the water will pour off and not onto my feet.

I put every piece of clothing in the dryer and flopped down on the bed. Everything was cold and humid (the French have apparently not yet discovered the wonders of heaters and dehumidifiers) but it didn't really matter—we were safe and sound.

And then I lost my merino sock. I should explain the significance of this loss. In my very limited stock, I possessed four pairs of socks. Two merino, two summer sport socks. The sport socks were solely to give extra padding to the merino ones on very wet days, or on days when I had sore tendons. I could not wear the sport socks alone as they were not thick enough and therefore wouldn't protect me against my blisters, Lucy and Bruce, who were always looking for an excuse to pop out their heads. So really, my most important socks were my two pairs of merinos and I cherished them more than life itself.

Do you want to walk the Camino? Then save your money. Have you saved it? Now go spend it all on socks. This is the best advice I can give anyone. The socks are what your most precious commodity, your feet, are going to be feeling. Day in, day out, good, wonderful, waterproof thick socks. There is no better tool on the road.

My merinos were that for me. They were my cushion, my warmth, my safety blanket. I had a ritual at the end of every day. Peel off your socks, wash them in warm soapy water, wring them out, hang them on the line. Pull out a new pair for the next morning. If the socks are not entirely dry by the time you need to start walking, no worries. Pin them to your bag and set out. The sun will take care of the rest. I did this every day on my 65-day trail. But I needed two pairs of socks. And now one of them was divorced.

I took everything out of the dryer and assembled them all in my bag. I double-checked, looked back in the dryer, behind the furniture, under the bed. Gone, gone, gone. No sock. We asked the other guests at the inn who had used the washing machine. Nadine and Patrice, who were doing the last ten-day stretch in France, and Jeanne and André, a Swiss couple who had been walking for two weeks, all pitched in and looked through the laundry. They offered their sympathies but no one had seen the sock.

It wasn't the worst thing that could happen on the road, but it did me in. After 20 miles of walking in the cold, wind and rain, getting lost in a tire yard, wearing a raincoat that cannot hold a candle to the one I'd lost and finishing the day in a cornfield with a crisis of constipation, the last thing I needed was to lose a favorite sock.

"My sock!" I sobbed, holding my head in my hands.

Nic patted my shoulders. "Come on, now, muffin."

"I just want my sock, I just want my sock! I loved it so much."

"Let me go look."

He went to the laundry room and emerged minutes later holding my beloved merino sock. "Clearly this trip has not improved your investigational skills." Camino miracle!

Camino Miracle

Chapter 17
Crunch, Ping!

One day I woke up, and I didn't want to walk. I was not particularly in any sort of pain, I was not homesick, and the weather was not too bad. I just didn't want to walk. I lay in bed, feeling like I'm three years old and about to throw a tantrum, "I WON'T go to daycare!!!" Except for me it was, "I WON'T walk another step!"

The previous night may have had something to do with my grumpy state of mind. I entered town limping once more on Bruce who had re-emerged with a vengeance. Blisters, again, this far into the trip! It was very hot and my sweaty feet were painful. I took off my sock and pulled out a needle and thread, ready to work on Bruce, who was bulging and big. "Here," says Nic, peering over my shoulder, "let me help." He says this as I am simultaneously piercing my skin. As if in slow motion, I watch in horror as a single jet stream of blister liquid exits my toe and sprays Nicolas in the face. I clap my hand over my mouth, fighting both the urge to cry and to laugh, and say, " Oh my goodness, Nicolas, I am so sorry. That was completely disgusting."

"I'll say," he replies, removing his glasses and wiping them clean. "Man, Jenna, even blisters are exciting with you." I feel my chin quiver. I am ready to cry with frustration.

"Aw, come on," he says, looking at me. "This is hysterical. And what are you crying about? You're not the one who just got sprayed with blister ooze."

And so I woke up the next morning, blisters dried out, but having lost my passion for walking. I just didn't feel like it. This apparently became my new obstacle: my distaste for the road. I was expecting the blisters, the reactions to bad water, the loneliness for my friends, the days of rain. But I wasn't expecting the total lack of interest in walking. It took me by surprise. I am supposed to strap on my bag, gulp down the pathetic piece of bread and cup of coffee the French call breakfast, fill up my bottle and be on my merry way. But what I really wanted to do was put on my slippers, stuff myself with eggs and bacon and watch "Sex and the City."

I tell Nic about my lack of motivation and he is annoyingly unsympathetic, "Well, that's your spiritual discipline. This isn't a vacation. It's a path of motivation and spiritual exercise. If you were here for tourism's sake, there would have been a heck of a lot easier ways to see some pretty countryside. Come on, let's get going. Move those little legs."

My spiritual discipline. I am uncomfortable with the notion. I still hadn't quite nailed down what my inner, ulterior motive for this walk was to be. Nicolas was convinced you needed a spiritual motivation to do it, because if you don't have one, it's just one long painful walk, at times through some not so pretty areas. The day before, about 80 percent of the road was on asphalt by the side of a highway. Awful. So I get that you need some reason to do the Camino besides wanting to take a hike through some cute scenery. I get that waking up every morning and going forward is part of the learning, but I am disinclined to call it a spiritual discipline.

Discipline. I hate the word. For me, it's synonymous with being punished when I was a child. A spanking was "discipline." Then as my sisters and I grew older, there was a transfer of the use of the word to something apparently positive—the spiritual disciplines, which in Christian households meant daily praying, reading the Bible, fasting. "How are your spiritual disciplines going?" my parents would ask us cheerfully, as though this would stimulate a positive conversation around the benefits of a rich inner world of prayer and Bible knowledge. The word, however, just evoked images of waiting on my bed while the adults decided my fate for having hit my sisters or lied to them.

You could say that I don't have the best rapport with the idea of discipline. My spiritual "disciplines," the odd times when I would remember to pray and read the Bible, were cultivated out of a guilty idea from my Christian circles that I didn't have a serious enough faith. And so the word has become somewhat tainted for me. Evangelicalism has a lovely way of doing that—tainting words. I have a friend who's a Unitarian. She told me that her minister calls this phenomenon "wounded words".

"Wounded words?" I ask.

"Well, my minister defines it as a word from religion that has been used to hurt us. Or a word that you love but whose definition has been abused by others. I think it can also be a word that's been used so negatively, that you can't use it for personal, positive use anymore because it evokes hurtful memories."

Curiously, I ask, " So what are the wounded words that your church has talked about?"

"Well let's see, there's faith ... and God."

I'm OK with faith. I'm all right with the word God. But I sense that the word discipline is my wounded word.

So I decided that I needed to reconcile myself to the idea of doing something repetitive and somewhat unpleasant without the associations of guilt and punishment that were passed down to me by the Church. That's one serious challenge. Challenge. Another word that the church owns. Usually used in the context of something bad going on in your life, just plain sucky, and then someone says, "God is challenging you", instead of, "Gee, that's crappy. Sorry."

Back to the walking. I put one leg in front of the other, feeling a mixture of boredom and annoyance. There were some pretty hills that day and some sweet 400-year-old buildings. I tried to feel enthralled, but I wasn't. The aesthetics of the road didn't hold their usual magic. That day, if I was going to feel good about the road, I would need to work on my mind and my inner contemplation.

Contemplation. Not a wounded word. A nice word. A peaceful word. So I began thinking, meditating and focusing through the repetitive motion of walking. One foot and then the next; not slow, not fast, just steady. The pebbles created a constant rhythmic sound that interacted with the clanging of my walking poles as they hit the ground—crunch, ping! Crunch, ping!

I was less than thrilled about walking today. But I reminded myself that I was not doing it out of guilt, nor was it punishment. The first thing was to become sternly honest with myself: The walking may be some form of suffering, but I chose it. I signed up for it. My body may be in pain, my soul fatigued, my mind bored, but this was all my doing. Was I really suffering? Girls sold into slavery are actually suffering. When my grandmother died, I suffered. But this path, this was only temporarily a bit tough.

Another thing about walking: I was certainly never as stressed while walking as I am when I'm at work. I'm very good at being stressed, it's something that I've mastered. I even dream about stresses at work. The other day I dreamt that I was at the airport trying to get on the plane, but I couldn't because there was a file that wouldn't leave my hand, and I needed to get it back to the office. It was a barely veiled message from my subconscious. There's a heaviness that I associate with my life in community work that seems to linger no matter how happy I am, no matter how well things are going at the job. It may be from the eternal phone calls, emails and deadlines, but even more, it is caused by being surrounded by so many sad stories.

Before I'd left we'd been dealing with one girl, Felicity, who kept returning to her abusive boyfriend. I know social workers who are amazingly agile at looking at a situation like that and leaving it at work, as if it were just a drippy faucet to be dealt with another time. I am notorious for letting sad stories scrape their nails across my heart as though it were a chalkboard.

So the walking lightened me. Being on the Camino created a forced separation from anything that normally would stress me out. There was not a thing in the world that I could do while walking the Camino to save Felicity. Truthfully, there never was, even when I was back at work and talking with her every day. If people want to remain out of the light, they will. Darkness can be a very fertile ground for stubborn behavior.

The walking looked after me, even on days when I didn't like walking. Whether I wanted it or not, my body was becoming healthier, my face taking in more sun, my legs becoming stronger, my mind less frazzled. The repetitive, unpleasant motion, the "crunch, ping," was doing good things for me, despite my feelings of annoyance. The walk was taking care of me, healing me, making me stronger overall.

The other marvelous thing about walking is that it is duty without guilt. You are not walking because you would feel guilty if you didn't. You are walking because if you don't, you won't get to your next destination. It's so simple. You'd miss out on seeing your Camino friends, you'd miss out on the path, your legs might begin to feel twitchy. Some days it did not feel like much of a choice, but a choice it was. I never walked because I would feel like a failure if I didn't. I never walked for fear of being judged. I walked to get to the next place.

Finally, that day, I moved into a mode of comfort with my walking, the sound of it centering my mind once more—crunch, ping! crunch, ping! The soft ground beneath my feet became my sacred space, the trees my fellow worshippers, the sun my companion. I put one foot in front of the next in a repetitive rhythm, leaning on my poles. I stopped thinking about how much I didn't like this, and began just focusing on one spot on the horizon. At one point, I realized I hadn't been thinking at all for the past hour. Breathe in, breath out. Crunch, ping! crunch, ping!

Crunch, Ping!

Chapter 18
Slower, Deeper, Meeker

We began hearing about pilgrims who were already days and days ahead of us even though we had started out at the same time.

"How do they do it?" I ask.

Our friend Yan shrugged his shoulders. "They eat while walking, they talk while walking, they only stop once in the whole day, they start out earlier and end later. I could probably do more, but my wife told me to pace myself. Remember how upset she was that I had arrived at the next stop before anyone else a few days ago? Well, now every time I call home she always makes sure I didn't do too many kilometers and that I wasn't the fastest walker. Apparently this is what I was supposed to learn on the road."

"So what is she, like your Camino coach?"

"Something like that ..."

"The pilgrimage could be an Olympic sport!" I say and Yan throws back his head and laughs.

"I am pretty sure," he says thoughtfully, "that the Olympic values of higher-faster-stronger are not the ones put forth by Saint-James. Not unless you were judged on how seriously you took the road—like how much thought you put into each step."

"So what, instead of higher-faster-stronger, it could be, maybe slower-deeper-meeker," I reply.

"Something like that. Impossible to judge really."

"OK, so the Olympic sport thing won't work."

"I doubt it."

Later on, I ask Nicolas whether or not he wished we were doing the walk faster.

"Well, if I wasn't walking with you, I'd probably be a good 60 miles ahead."

I wince. "Sorry."

"No, I didn't mean that in a bad way. The slowness is probably good for me. It gave me time to connect with people, it made me put aside my drive. Besides, without you I'd be lonely."

"Happy to help!" I pat his hand. "And, if it wasn't for you, I'd be behind. And I might have taken a whole lot more days off. I'd probably be running out of money. And there'd be no one to comfort me when I lose my stuff."

"Well," Nic says, treading carefully (as he always does when I am rightfully self-critical), "You help me remember people's names ..."

This is true. He's a disaster when it comes to names. We play the name game to keep us occupied on the road. It goes something like this:

"OK, nice Swiss man we had breakfast with this morning?"

"Georges!"

"Nope, his name is André. What's his wife's name? You guys talked for an hour yesterday about whale watching in Tadoussac."

"Umm ... Karine?"

"Nope again. Jeanne. How about the Frenchman from Lyon that just passed us by?"

"Samuel?"

"Nicolas, seriously, we slept in the same room as him for three nights in a row! His name is Daniel."

"Aaargh!"

But back to doing the Camino together. Nic says, "I'd be getting there faster but I'd be lost to myself. Lonely, I mean. And I wouldn't know what to do with my frustrations. So I wouldn't be peaceful. Calm."

"So the slowness is good?"

"As long as we can keep leaving early, yeah ... the slowness is good."

Life is slow on the road. I can hardly believe that I spend a minimum of five hours each day—usually it's more like seven or eight—simply walking. At home, I watch TV, cook and research stuff on the computer all at the same time. I can't multitask on the road. I just walk. Me and my soul, my mind, my memories. Sure, I talk to people. Sure, I have Nicolas. But there really is a whole lot of empty time.

Back home, a friend told me, "I wouldn't be able to do what you're going to do."

"Oh, I'm certain you could," I started to say. "You're in good health. If you started training, you'd be fine."

"No, I mean spiritually and psychologically. I can't be alone with my thoughts for all those days. I'm not ready for that yet. It would be turmoil and pain. I'd need at least another three years of therapy before I can get to that point. But hey, what's life without goals?"

"Right," I say, surprised at her candor. And then I began wondering whether or not I was ready for all that time alone, with no distractions, no neurotic friends by whom I could measure my own levels of emotional balance and mental health, no TV shows to turn to in my moments of panic and stress, no therapist waiting for my next crisis, just a phone call away.

"Your mind is like a bad neighborhood," someone quoted Anne Lamott to me once. "You shouldn't go in there alone."

Well, I was going in alone. I was going to go deep. Depth can be a scary thing. It is supposed to be a positive thing like when you talk about someone who is reflective and thoughtful and you say of this person, "She is so deep." On the other hand, if a scuba diver goes too many feet down, she can begin to lose pressure and oxygen control. So depth can be bad. My depth on the Camino came in slowness, in the walking,

Most mornings when dark thoughts decided to reveal themselves, it would always be in the form of worry. I worried about the staff I left behind in May. I worried about whether or not they're OK, if the center was falling apart without me, if they were having any problems with the alarm, if the grant money from the city had come in yet. I worried about every little thing out of my control.

I worried about my pregnant sister and those terrible, steep stairs descending from our inner-city apartment building, and that she might fall down them and lose the baby. I worried about our cat and that he would get terribly lonely and die of starvation.

I worried about the kids at the center.

I think I worry about them more than they do about themselves. I worry about them, probably, more than their own parents do.

The latest kid I was worrying about is Alison. Alison is a wild child and she is beloved by all at the center. She is beautiful. Not just beautiful like all kids have some beauty. No, Alison has chocolate-smooth skin and cat eyes and full lips and she exudes beauty. She has a smoky voice with a natural singing talent and a bright and curious mind. She also drives people crazy, is totally self-destructive and has blown every chance ever given to her for happiness and health.

"That child," I told my colleague once, "is allergic to the light. There is no other way for me to say it."

She had had a hard childhood, getting bumped from foster home to foster home. Finally at the age of 16 she moved in with her possessive and abusive boyfriend. I'd receive the odd phone call at work with her sobbing into the phone at the bus stop, telling me about the latest fight And how he had hit her.

She'd come in and we'd feed her and tell her about the shelters and services. "Just say the word, Alison. We can go today and move you out. Just say the word."

She never said the word.

Every technique, every boundary, every form of intervention was used on her. She'd been tough loved, prayed for, encouraged, comforted, corrected and counseled. But Alison's worst enemy, was, well, Alison. "How to pin a wave upon the sand," is the phrase that comes to mind. If Alison would only let me be in charge of her life, everything would be Ok. At least, that's what I think when I'm feeling out of control. We'd get her moved out and serious about school. She would quit going back to destructive, rotten men, and dangerous, manipulative friends. We'd get her off drugs and out of pimping rings and into a career that would really help her blossom.

But that isn't the way. I am sure that God must have those moments with me. "Aaargh, if she would only let me be in charge, her life would go so much better." But it's all about letting those we love make their own choices, isn't it?

There's nothing like youth work to make you feel sorry for God. Truly, I empathize.

So Alison was popping into my head these days. The fact is she may fail her June exams, stay with the mean boyfriend, never get her life organized, and float from one bad situation to another. I'm not being cynical, I'm being realistic. But every now and again, I think about this, and my chest tightens up and I think through every mistake I made with Alison, all those times I didn't have the right words, that maybe I should have pushed harder to get her out of that house. If I had tightened the rules around her schoolwork, maybe things would have gone better.

Maybe.

I could float on an ocean of maybes, could-haves, would-haves, should-haves, until my worries carry me out to sea and leave me stranded on a desert island of guilt and second-guessing.

So I reminded myself that these are dark thoughts and I start whispering the names and things that are causing me grief.

Today, it's Alison.

"Alison, Alison, Alison, Alison."

This is the way. I cannot control what happens with Alison. And so I speak her name to the Higher Power, the only One who has any control over anything, and I pray that I will forgive myself for my mistakes and that I will remember in Whose hands Alison's life is.

I speak her name in prayer, and my chest begins to relax.

There was one morning when it was the names of my staff. Hmm, I thought, why am I worried about them? And the ritual returned.

"Names and names and names and names ..." over and over again.

When I got back home, Ève, my colleague told me about an especially bad period in June when Caroline, our teacher, fell very sick with pneumonia and wound up in intensive care for several days. Having the director gone on sabbatical and a staff member in ICU meant that the remaining staff (all one and a half of them) went into major overdrive. "Life went on," she shrugged. Blessed girl!

I asked her in what week all of that had happened. When she told me, I did a mental calculation and nodded, "I was very worried about you all that week. I think that's when I began praying your names."

Ève stared at me. "Did it help?"

"It helped me. Caroline's pneumonia might have another opinion."

"Well, we're in one piece, aren't we?"

"That you are. Thanks for not telling me when it was all going on."

She stared at me again, as if this were the strangest thing I could have said. "Jenna, you were on a pilgrimage somewhere in southern France. What was I going to do, tweet you and say, 'Could you take a break from the monks and help us answer some emails, because the office is really bogged down right now?'"

"Thanks, nonetheless."

Ève raised such a lovely point. I was always under the impression that if I could just keep a handle on everything, I would be a strong director. I've had to learn how little I can control, how little any of us can control. Rob Bell writes in *Velvet Jesus*, "Sabbath is a day a week where I am reminded that I did not create the world and it will continue to exist without my efforts."

If one day a week should and can do that, try three months. There is guilt and anxiety to wade through, worries about your cat, your money, your staff, your pregger sister living on the third floor, the stupidity-prone kids that you minister to. But once all that passes, there is pure and utter holy euphoria. God lets you know your efforts are not always needed. I wonder if God had to work this out on His day of rest. Would the Siberian Cranes remember to migrate east in time? Would the sea turtles figure out they needed to come up for air approximately once every five hours? But rest He did, all the same. And so I rest. And in resting, I give up control.

"I am not in control" is now my mantra of choice.

This is meekness.

On the Camino, I would be overwhelmed with the desire to snap back into motion and start gathering people, duties, memos, meetings and hold them all clumsily in my arms in order to keep some semblance of power. "What if" became the question of choice at the beginning. What if things go wrong? What if so-and-so doesn't show up for their exam? What if the money doesn't come in, the toilet breaks, my sister falls down the steps, our apartment gets robbed? And God said, "Yes, that could happen. Your colleague may fall gravely ill, wind up in the hospital, the center may go to pieces for a time. The 'what ifs' may come true. You know what you can do about it? Not a single thing."

Allison, as I found out when I came back, could not have been doing worse. She didn't show up for any exams, thus failing her entire school year, her bad-boyfriend was still very much in the picture, and if the latest rumors are true, and usually they are, she was earning a living by pole dancing. The idiom, " It'll all turn out for the best" really does not apply here. It's a heartbreaking, soul-groaning, head-snapping slap of crappy reality. Not everything turned out OK. But even if had been around, things would not have turned out any better. In fact, I'd probably have been spinning on myself in a frenzy of self-obsessed stress.

By respecting the Sabbath, I removed myself from the equation. And meekness set in. Actively. It was strong and powerful, and I felt strength within me as I heard all sorts of bad news.

Slowness brought me to depth. Depth made me think. But meekness was where I really worked. Accept the "what ifs." I am not in control. Meekness became my strength. Meekness became my fallback mantra. Meekness reminded me of what I am, which is to say, someone who is simply trying to keep still while riding the waves of all the things that could drown us.

Chapter 19
Mark

"So," says Nadine, our latest walking friend, to us one morning, "have you met Mark?"

"Not yet," I reply, "but I've heard about him."

"Patrice and I were quite worried about him. He hadn't had a square meal in days. But maybe that's just our middle-age talking and we have lost touch with your generation."

"Well," I say, "apparently this kid has been walking as much as any of us and eating considerably less, so I'd say he's the one who's lost touch, not you."

"That's a lovely way of making me feel young!" Nadine laughs. "I'll see you tonight in Arroue."

"Save me a piece of Basque cake if I arrive later than you."

That day, we met Mark. We were walking, or rather sloshing, along a very wet path on our second day into the Pyrenees region. The sun was beginning to break out, thankfully.

"Hello," he says.

"Hello." Young, unwashed and redheaded, he looked a little out of place amongst all the upper-class French retirees. No wonder Nadine was perplexed.

"How long have you been walking?" Nicolas asked.

"About three weeks. I flew into Paris from Prague. That's where I'm from, Prague. I tried couch surfing in Paris, but the people I'd arranged with were out of town. So I walked the town on that first night, and then hitchhiked down to Le Puy."

"How did you manage the rain yesterday?" I asked, peering at his tattered bag and clothes.

"Well, I asked the innkeeper if I could sleep in his barn, and he gave me his tent. But what with the rain coming down so hard all night, I really couldn't sleep. It's like sleeping with a marching band above your head! It's OK, though, I mean, it was free."

"So you're doing this old school then?" I ask.

"What's this 'old school?'"

"It means the way Medieval pilgrims who had no money used to do it. Walking from village to village working on the farm for room and board."

"Well, yes. I've been trying to find work, but there isn't much. A man back in Lauzertes offered to have me do maintenance for two weeks at the town inn, but not for pay. Just for a bed to sleep in."

"The economy isn't very good right now."

"I know. I'm hoping in Spain things will be better. I'll try and find work there."

"Do you speak Spanish?" asks Nicolas.

"No."

"Mark, you do realize that the unemployment rate in Spain is 20 percent right now, don't you?"

"Really?"

"Really."

"Huh."

We walked on. Mark told us how before leaving, he broke up with his girlfriend, quit his job, closed down his apartment and put everything in a storage locker. He was, for all intents and purposes, homeless. We took a rest about an hour later, and he pulled a box of chocolates from his bag and offered us some.

"A very nice lady in a bakery gave these to me two days ago. They've been my food for the road." I nod and hand him an apple in exchange. "You probably need some fruit." I said. He nodded.

We walked along further and saw some sheep in a pasture. He walked up towards a barbed fence and peered at some sheep's wool hanging off the barbs in strings and clumps.

"What are you doing?" I questioned him.

"Well, sheep's wool, when you wrap it around your toes, helps heal and prevent blisters. I don't want to buy any at the pharmacy, so ..."

I looked at the dirty wool he was holding in his hands and thought about it rubbing up against an open wound.

"Oh, my goodness," I thought to myself. "This kid is going to die on the road. He could actually keel over from blood poisoning and die."

I fought the urge to do as I would with one of the kids from the center: Step in, and try to stop them from doing something incredibly stupid. I chose not to stop Mark. First, I am not at work. Second, Mark is making his own choices. Bad choices they may be, but they're choices all the same. He's thought this through and decided to travel this way.

Third, and maybe most importantly, I'm tired. It's hard enough taking care of one's own self on the road, without having to care for someone else's safety. In this sense, the generosity of hosts and priests and townspeople is needed. Pilgrims can be kind, some of them exceedingly self-sacrificing (there are all sorts of beautiful anecdotes about people stopping on the road to lend a necessary, sometimes life-saving hand), but ultimately you are responsible for yourself and your immediate companions. I just didn't have it in me to care for this self-made vagabond.

We arrived at our destination. Basque houses on the horizon dotted the mountain. "What will you do for accommodations tonight?" Nicolas asked Mark.

"I will either go to the office of tourism—they're pretty good at pointing you in the direction of donativo residences, you know, the ones by donation—or I'll go to the church and ask the priest if I can sleep there."

"OK, then. Good luck, Mark."

We walked off towards our inn. "What do you make of that?" I asked Nic.

"Weird guy. I'm glad there's a space for him on the Camino, but I'm also glad there's only one of him. Can you imagine if everyone did their pilgrimage like him?"

"There wouldn't be a Camino left to do. The villagers would run us out of town with knives and pitchforks."

We were quiet for a bit. Then Nicolas laughed. "Finding work in Spain! It's like trying to find a real breakfast in France. Can't be done."

Chapter 20
Last Days in France

During my last days in France, I fit into the road like my hands in a glove. We took off in the morning, bags on our backs as if we were carrying no more than a pound or two. I walked 16 miles with no more effort than if I were walking to the corner store for a pint of milk. My feet didn't hurt anymore. I had gotten so used to the terrain, the weather, the ground, and the distances that walking came naturally to me.

This was the sweetest of times, and the saddest, knowing that our time in France would soon be over and that once more, the lovely batch of friends we'd made would be parting ways with us. Célia and Robert were the only ones still around who'd started out on the same day as us. We'd made new friends, most of whom would end their trek in a day or two. We would be going on and they would not. Even Yan, my beloved Dutchman, had said goodbye to us the night before.

"So," I said to him, "your wife couldn't convince you to go all the way to Santiago?"

"She was a hell of a Camino coach," he smiled, "but what can I say? I miss my kids. My daughter called me last night in hysterics because her boyfriend texted her that there was a math exam the next day that she didn't know about. And through all her sobs and declarations of her life failures, I thought, I miss the teenage drama."

I gave him a hug and bought him a pint. "Thanks for telling me about all your work troubles and stresses. It made me feel like I wasn't alone."

"You know more about me now than some colleagues I've had for 13 years. But, Jenna, you're too young to be under the same stresses as me. I had twenty years to build up to my burnout. And now, I think, I didn't need to freak out like I did. It wasn't that bad!"

I shrugged my shoulders. "I don't know what the answer is for me, Yan. I don't think it's a change of career or a burnout."

Yan laughed. "No, that's not your answer. Go back to your work. Love what's good. Forget about the rest." I nodded and waved goodbye, knowing I'd miss him.

It was a sad goodbye, but the ambiance was so good on the road these days. We were definitely in the Pyrenees region, getting views of the mountains and lush, grassy valleys at every twist and turn in the road. It was a beautiful peace and a jovial existence of companies, where we knew our fellow walkers and celebrated with them these last moments of their journeys. We had sing-a-longs at night and long coffee breaks in the middle of the day. The breaking-in of the road was over. Now it was party time.

On our last full day of walking in France, we left at an easy hour after two coffees and extra bread at breakfast.

"Do you reckon Spain will have something that more closely resembles a real breakfast?" I asked Nic.

"Baby, it couldn't be much worse than here."

Nadine, who'd been joined at the hip with us ever since we'd met her a week back, came down to the table. "Bonjour, les jeunes," she said in a cheery tone. "Do you think it will rain? There seem to be some clouds."

"Oh, I don't think so," replied Nic.

Nadine laughed. "Nicolas, you are the ray of sunshine around here. You see clouds, it won't rain; you see a long road, it won't be so bad; you meet someone rude, you say maybe they're just having a bad day. The glass is always half full!"

I listened to Nadine's description of my husband and looked at him quizzically.

"You know," said Nic, "at home, I am quite the pessimist."

Nadine and her husband Patrice stopped in their tracks, "Non! This can't be true. You're being hard on yourself."

"No, really, he's a pain in the butt," I offered up.

Nadine thought for a moment, "Well, then, the road has served you well."

We tied our shoes, hoisted our packs onto our backs and took off. We were still deep in Basque country, with the rust-red roofs of houses peaking out everywhere, sheep baa-ing in every field, men with weathered faces and rough hands holding pipes and tipping their woolen berets when you passed them on the road. We reached our day's mid-point and stopped for lunch.

"I feel tired today. I think it's because my body knows I'm up for a break," said Nic. I looked at the clock inside the bar.

"There's only about an hour and a half left till we get to St-Jean Pied de Port. We've made fantastic time."

"There you are!" I heard a voice behind us. It was Nadine. "André has been watching the two of you walk so fast all morning. He said you were in a hurry to find yourselves back in the intimacy of your bedroom."

"Nadine!" I exclaimed, laughing embarrassingly.

"I didn't say that, mind you, it was André. I am only telling you because I am honest."

The table besides us were laughing. Nic shook his head, "Ah, the French."

"I am not French, I am Swiss." André said, pulling up a chair. "Don't be embarrassed, les petits canadiens. A young couple in love is a beautiful thing."

"André is very philosophical today," piped in Nadine.

"Thank you, Nadine. You too, I have found, are very deep. Today at least."

"It doesn't happen often," said her husband Patrice. "We must take advantage of it while it lasts."

"Honestly!" said Nadine, only slightly fake-annoyed. "Everyone is in such a mood today."

"Last day on the road in France," said Nic. "It's like the last day of school. No more discipline. We're off. Let's not talk dirty about ourselves while we're out. Don't let your imaginations run too wild."

A little while later, we stood in front of the gated city of Saint-Jean Pied-de-Port. We walked up the stone walkway and stood under the huge Medieval arches. I had a lump in my throat. We had reached the end of France.

"We're here," said Nic.

I nodded. Nicolas put his arm around me and we stood still for a moment. We clicked away the must-have photos and found our lodgings, an easy task as Saint-Jean consists of no more than two main streets and a canal. Later in the afternoon I found the rest of our walker group and began to say goodbye to them. They would be continuing next year, or not at all. For most of them, Saint-Jean was the destination. I corralled André, Jeanne, Nadine and Patrice and we decided to eat together. A last supper.

Supper times were one of my favorite parts of the road in France. Rarely less than three courses, home cooked, bountiful and rustic, the meals provided hours of table time in which the pilgrims bonded together over a communion of food and wine. After a day of walking in the scorching heat or the frigid rain, the supper table was sacred ground, the dinner guests its dutiful parishioners. That last night we found ourselves in a traditional Basque restaurant, and we immediately pulled three tables together. God forbid that we not have one long table for our final meal.

"What's been the lesson of the Camino for the two of you so far?" Nadine asked us.

"I'm not sure," I said, thinking hard. "But one thing is, we've had to come to an acceptance of each other. We walk so differently. Nic is always ahead of me, so comfortable on the road. I lag behind, trying to find my pace, wanting to stop to eat, you know, all of that. We've had to work to find each other's company on the road."

"Yes," said Patrice, "we noticed that. We have a nickname for Nicolas."

"What's that?" Nicolas asked.

"First, I must tell you a story. When we first set out, there was a man and his wife whom we met who'd already been walking some time. They decided to do the Camino with a donkey."

"Really?" I asked. "Why so?"

"For transporting their equipment. They'd been going for a long time, so they really needed more than a backpack. Well, in any case, it turns out the donkey had a very good sense of hearing. He'd walk on ahead with the husband, but categorically if they got too far ahead, the donkey would stop and refuse to go on until he could hear the wife's footsteps. And he got quite good at recognizing her footsteps. If it was anyone else behind him, he wouldn't start walking again, he'd simply wait for her."

"That's amazing. And sweet."

"Quite. And so you see, we call Nicolas your donkey." Nicolas and I smirked. "He's grown accustomed to waiting for me," I said affectionately.

"She's getting better at keeping her pace," Nic joined in. "But I still have to wait."

"So, everyone?" asked André. "Here we are, at the end of one journey, our friends about to continue on. What have you learned about yourselves?"

"I am amazed that I could live off of one outfit," said Nadine.

"I am amazed that I could be without my phone and TV," says Jeanne.

"I am amazed at the lack of choice," said Nic. "Every day, you don't have a choice about what hour you will get up. You wake up when everyone else does."

"You don't choose the trail," added Patrice. "If you want to get to the next place on your destination, you have to follow the road mapped out for you."

"You don't choose your lodgings," I said, "Most of the time, the towns only had one inn, maybe two or three if you were lucky. There wasn't a panoply of accommodations."

"You don't choose your meal," said André. "No menu for dinner. Just take what the hostess gives you."

"We aren't any worse for wear, though, are we?" asked Jeanne.

André lifted his glass. "Friends, generalized comfort leads to the dwindling of hopes. I shall always cherish the simplicity and discomfort of the Camino."

Chapter 21
Crossing Over

On the morning when we would leave France and cross over into Spain, we woke up late. We only had five miles to do, albeit at a frightening ascent, and we now knew our way in and around town, having spent the previous day navigating its multiple streets and alleys.

We started our hike deep into the Pyrenees and I began to gorge myself on scenery. Everywhere I looked there were paths and trails carved into lush green and majestic mountains. Boulders larger than life, hills, meadows, rocky terrains and steep green and violet walls of forest surrounded us. I was taking it all in in a most desperate manner. I was gasping at the beauty of it all, but not silenced by it one bit. No, rather I was panicking that I won't see enough, I was mourning all the paths I would not walk, clicking my camera away furiously, terrified that the moment would pass, that I wouldn't see and feel enough of these views.

"Calm down," I kept telling myself, annoyingly. This was exactly what I was trying to work against on the Camino: the inability to root myself in the present and feel gratitude for what was going on right then and there. My mind was already days ahead, feeling sad that I wouldn't be in the Pyrenees anymore. Then my head was days behind, missing the people whom we said goodbye to. I was worried we wouldn't spend enough time hiking the beautiful mountains.

"Stop it!" my inner voice commanded. "Maybe you won't ever see this again. So what? You'll have seen it today."

And see it I did, finally. I put the camera away. We stopped on the side of the road and sipped water. I admired the wildflowers growing on the side of a cliff. We walked some more, then stopped and Nicolas took one picture of a cloud covering a mountain peak. I took in the view and then turned and walked on. We stopped to watch some mountain goats and ponies. Lovely. We listened to the cowbells echoing in the distance. I sipped more water. Time slowed. I turned my face toward the bright sun and blue sky.

Houses were sparse, so we played our usual guessing game, "How do the people live?" We mused at how they possibly survived winter blizzards and whether or not they were able to live off the profits from their cattle. We arrived at our B & B around noon, in far better shape than all the newbies surrounding us who were only just beginning their Camino. "Wow," said Nic looking around at all the out-of-breath, heavy-laden new pilgrims. "Remember our first day?"

"Thirty days ago now. Do you think we smell really bad?"

"Your over-developed sense of smell is the bane of my Camino existence."

He had a point. We'd had enough hot days lately that I'd taken to sniffing my clothes, my bag straps, my head bandana in a nearly obsessive manner.

"Come on, let's sit."

The inn of Orisson had cleverly built its main eating area on an elevated terrace that overlooked a beautiful setting of mountainous landscapes, green pastures and herds of wooly sheep. The view and ambiance compensated for the moldy rooms and impossible host, a 40-something, rough-mannered, outspoken Basque man who thought far too highly of himself and his premises.

Nicolas and I sat all afternoon on the terrace with Célia and Robert, and took in the sights. I stopped mourning the fact that by tomorrow, I would no longer be here.

We looked around and established the fact that there were hardly any more French people. There were, however, many other nationalities represented. "It's a change from the homogenous French 50-plussers we've been walking with, isn't it?" I asked Nic.

"Please, I never thought I'd have so much knowledge about pension plans in France."

"Where are all the French?" I asked Célia.

"In France. Don't you know they hate leaving their own territory? How many times did someone tell you the prettiest scenery would be behind you once you cross over to Spain? Or how you should enjoy the food while you can, because in Spain it will be atrocious? The French acknowledge that there is life outside of France, but they are none too pleased by that fact."

At suppertime we met new people. All new people. They'd just finished their first day of walking. A father from Italy with his son and daughter. A mother from Philadelphia with her teenage daughter. A couple from Quebec and their mother. A family from Spain. A 30-something woman from Israel. We told them this is Day 32 for us and we watched their jaws drop. The questions began. What do you do about blisters? How much weight is in your bag?

"Hey, I remember these conversations," I said. I enjoyed being the knowledgeable one at the table, for once. But I stopped myself from giving too much advice. "Everyone must figure out their own style on the Camino," I said serenely. I paused for a second and then added, "But, seriously, go pick up some alcohol swabs and a few cushioned Band-Aids."

The next morning, we peaked at the Pyrenees. The weather can change drastically and dangerously in these parts. There are stories about heavy fog setting in so thickly that pilgrims must stop where they are for fear of wandering off the trail. When the fog lifts, they find themselves in the middle of a cow field, or worse, in some forgotten ditch far away from civilization. Local rescue teams consisting of neighboring shepherds and milk farmers will go out to find lost hikers, bringing along a rope and a whistle. The whistle is so that they can find each other through the fog. The rope is attached to the hiker so he will be able to follow them. Sometimes lagging behind even five feet can have deadly consequences.

And that's just the fog. April and May have been known to bring blizzards and cold storms so violent that a pilgrim will freeze to death in his own tracks. In one section, there is a security shed set up with a wood stove and an emergency phone for these situations. The lucky ones will make it to this little one-room stone house.

This day, there was just a bit of cloud and fog, enough to make the greens stand out and the land to look a bit wispy and mysterious. We arrived at a small crossing; it was a narrow road surrounded by woods, with a water tap to the left. "Fontaine de Roland," read the inscription overhead. Roland, the iconic figure of minstrel culture from the "Chanson de Roland" is big in these parts, apparently. His victory under Charlemagne is retold in folklore. Legend has it that when he met the enemy in battle he drew his sword and struck the earth, creating ruptures in the ground and an avalanche of boulders, hence the reason we have the French-Spanish Pyrenees. Under the fountain, there was a metal grate on the ground that we walked over.

"I think we're in Spain," said Nicolas.

"Oh," I said and looked behind me. "Ok, then. Hello, Spain."

Book 2
Spain

Chapter 22
Espagna!

The only problem is, I don't speak Spanish. And nobody here speaks French or English. And everything closes from about 2:30 to 5:30 p.m. (Apparently the Spanish dislike work even more than the French.) Also, we arrived here on Pentecost Monday, which is apparently an important religious holiday in Spain meaning that cafés and stores are open even less than usual. And to top it off, our Casa Rural—a Spanish Bed and Breakfast, essentially—has the wrong address listed in the guide, sending us to a very nice man's private dwelling who attempts to turn us in the right direction, in Spanish, with us saying the occasional "Si, si."

We finally arrive at our lodgings and a very nice, very chipper girl shows us to our room—a room for two, comfortable sheets and oh, my stars above, there are clean white towels.

In a pilgrim's existence, there is perhaps no happier thing to discover than clean white towels in her room. When you normally only have a 10-square-inch camping towel to wipe yourself with every day, the occasional clean, fluffy, life-size terry cloth is welcomed with open arms.

I manage, with signs and my extensive three-word Spanish vocabulary, to ask for a clothesline.

Espagna!

We stay our first night in Burguete. Most walkers stay at the Monastery of Roncesvalles, right at the foot of the Spanish Pyrenees. We were advised by Nadine, in France, not to do this.

"The first couple of days in Spain will be a far cry from the quiet evenings at the French inns," she said. "You will be struck by the throngs of people at Roncesvalles. Don't worry, it thins out after the first week. But on your first night in Spain, go to Burguete. You will have a luxury of choices of Bed and Breakfasts and as many restaurants to match."

So go to Burgete we did. Her last statement would have been true had it not been for Pentecost Monday.

Burguete's claim to fame is that Ernest Hemingway vacationed here in 1924 and 1925. He was mesmerized with the Basque people, applauding their bullfighting and wine drinking. He wrote about the town in his novel, *The Sun Also Rises*. The protagonist and his mate stay in Burgete and spend five days trout-fishing in the Irati River, another great Basque sport.

The streets are the most amazing thing about this small town. There are miniature canals that run up and down each sidewalk for the water filtration. No matter where you walk, you will find water running down stones. The town also wakes up every morning to the quiet swoosh, step and cling! of the pilgrims' parade through their streets, the main road leading directly onto the path towards Pamplona. The soundtrack of the walkers has been part of their cultural tapestry for centuries, as much as the views of the Pyrenees from their backyard or the miniature canals.

The first two days in Spain, we are surrounded by pink hills and green olive plantations, vineyards and herb gardens. We'd been smelling sheep and cow manure for so long that when we arrived in Spain, the odors hit me in a surprising wave. Thyme, roses, eucalyptus, rosemary and lemon trees. This is what I smell all day long.

We stop one morning right before Pamplona and look at the table in front of us. The props are all right: walking poles, canvas backpacks, guide books on the chairs. But the people are so different compared to

France. "Good grief," I whisper to Nic, "we're no longer the youngest ones in the place."

"I feel like I've walked into a student association party," he replies, eyes wide.

When we arrive in Pamplona, around our third day in Spain, we line up at the *refugio* which is an old monastery with 40-bed dormitories. The money we save we'll spend on food and wine.

Nicolas has been socializing with a couple of Australian hikers, and a Canadian girl named Ann, and jogs back to our bed bunk. "Jen, you won't believe this, but the guys and Ann over there asked us if we want to meet up later and go drinking. Drinking, Jenna, in the bars! Like real self-respecting 20-somethings."

"You're no longer 20-something. And we drank plenty in France."

"Yeah, but in a more poetical manner. These guys are offering a night on the town ..."

I feel my shyness kick in. "Do we have to?"

"Let me put it this way. If we don't go out with the guys, we will be usurped by Robert and Célia who will spend the night talking about the pleasures of middle-age retirement funds and the impacts of their children's spoiled upbringings."

"I'll swing by the bank and pull out some euros," I say, climbing off the bed. I am fiercely loyal to Célia, as she has been with us since day one, and she offered her fair share of comfort and consolation when my blisters, Lucy and Bruce, were fired up and at their worst, but having a night out with a younger crowd did seem awfully appealing.

We meet up that night with a bunch of rowdy, laughing, wide-eyed 20-somethings, and I realize that we're part of the older ones. We tell everyone that we've been walking for 35 days and I begin to enjoy the questions they asked with awe and admiration.

"How did you manage the blisters?" asks Ann, and shows off her heels, swollen and puffy.

"Do you miss home?"

"Your calves must be strong ..."

I resist the temptation to tell people what they're doing wrong: Too much weight on one walker and another's plans to do 24 miles tomorrow are just downright masochistic. Ann is in bad need of some new socks. But I won't begin bossing people around. They'll find their own way. The Camino is a great propeller of surrender and concession.

"So," says Nic gulping down some wine, "how does eating and drinking work in this town?"

"Tapas runs," replies Sean. Sean is an Irish hiker who did the Camino last year. He serves as a reference guide for all those doing it for the first time.

"Tapas what?"

"Tapas runs. Have you noticed there is no possible way to get a decent meal around suppertime here? It's because people dine after nine. The best way to eat at a pilgrim's hour is to go up and down the street, bar to bar and gorge on tapas." Sean stuffs his face with an olive and prosciutto. He lifts his wine glass, "Buen Camino!"

"Buen Camino!!" everyone in the bar cheers and gulps. It turns out the Camino blessing has been co-opted into a drinking game.

"Hey, it's our two Canadian walkers!" I turn around and see Mia and Natalie. We met Mia and Natalie in the Pyrenees. They are a mother-daughter walking team, and I hasten to tell them that we had had very good experiences with mother-daughter combos, thinking back fondly to my encounters in the bushes with Jane and Kit.

"How did you hear about the Camino?" asks Nic.

"We have a house in Barcelona," replies Natalie, "and my grandparents are Spanish, so we've always known about it. But I decided this was the year to try it out. I turned 40 this year. Mia's going to be 15 in a few weeks, probably right around the time we reach Santiago."

"So you're 14," I say admiringly. "I wonder what it's like to be a teenager on this walk."

"You have to be pretty entertaining," Natalie whispers to me. "The contemplation aspect is a little much for a 14-year–old. Thank God for her iPhone. And reminding her to wear the elastics for her braces has quickly become the bane of my Camino." Mia grins at us.

"We've already dumped some weight from our bags," says Mia proudly, "and our favorite Camino item, bar none, is the urinator."

"May I commend you on mastering the use of that gadget," I say, pushing aside a few bad memories. "Truly, I am full of admiration."

Natalie goes on to tell us that she has two other daughters, aged 8 and 10 who have stayed home with her husband. It was obviously difficult for her to leave her kids behind for so long. She compensates by daily Skype calls home and frequent picture exchanges. The girls and her family follow their walk, step by step.

"You have to do this trail for a reason," declares Natalie with conviction, "if you're going to leave behind such precious commodities."

Later, much later, Natalie would tell us about her family business's difficulties during the economic crisis of 2008. She would tell us about her father's bouts of bad health, her eldest daughter moving to boarding school, her own personal existential crisis of needing to find a career for herself after not having worked in years. In the space of twelve months, her world had been rattled to its core. Everything she thought was airtight—money, status, family—had been shaken.

Reasons for doing the Camino? She had about 48. Camino question? More like Camino questions, plural. Life had thrown her more than one curve ball, all in the matter of a single year. She decided to walk 500 miles to try and shake of the shock. We didn't know all this on that evening in Pamplona. We didn't know the pain and the uncertainties that were propelling forward those two pairs of inexperienced legs. When I found out, it answered a few questions. But it mostly built up my respect for these two seemingly upper-middle class Americans with charmed lives. Every soul on the road has a story.

"So," continues Natalie, "35 days! You must have already met many people along the Way."

"Yes," I reply wistfully, "and said goodbye to a great many. Only Robert and Célia have continued on with us." I think nostalgically about Marius, Yan and Albert, Chantal and Nadine.

"And now you are making all sorts of hellos!" replies Mia.

"Yes," I smile and sip some wine, "there is always a new hello."

Chapter 23
Granddad

The next day, my last in Pamplona, I got the email about my grandfather. I can see the square—the Plaza del Castillo—and Nicolas and I are sitting on a terrace and drinking beer. It is a small wonder that I got the email because there have been so many villages recently that haven't had any Internet access. Thankfully, Pamplona is entirely wireless.

My mother wrote, "Hi honey. Granddad took a bad fall and had to be brought to the hospital. One thing led to another and it looks like he's got kidney failure. Your aunts and I have been on constant communications with the nursing home staff and because of his DNR (Do Not Resuscitate), they have removed antibiotics but have upped his liquids and painkillers. From last news, he's somewhat comatose. Jenna, I want you to walk a day for him and I know that you said your goodbyes to him last January. I am glad you did that visit. I am at peace."

I looked at the screen of our iPad and thought, "So that's it." I was very sure that my grandfather would pass away during my Camino experience. I had many moments up to that point on the road when I would stop and think, "Is Granddad dead?" because it just felt that real. So the email came and I wasn't that shocked.

Granddad

I looked out onto the square. The enormous Plaza del Castillo is beautiful. Real estate must be pricey. There are stone pathways, green squares, a large white gazebo and plenty of cafes with white and yellow-striped parasols installed over marble tables. We probably paid more for a pint of beer at the Plaza than in other places around the city, but no matter. We paid for the view.

We walked down the street where in only three weeks' time they'll be celebrating San Fermin, and loads of drunken college boys will be racing the bulls, some may be trampled to death, others only slammed against the red walls of old stone buildings, if they're lucky.

I wonder if I'll cry. I tell Nicolas who takes my hand and asks if I want to call home. Yes. I do want to call home. I haven't shed a tear yet, and I know why.

Because I've already cried.

My trip in January was with my mother down to the Pennsylvania town where her parents had lived for the past twenty years. As they aged from young seniors to functional seniors to dependent seniors, it had become increasingly difficult to figure out what the best plan of care should be. My grandmother is—how can I put this lightly?—difficult. And I mean that in the worst possible way. My grandfather is—how can I say this?—mild. And I mean that in the most victimizing sense of the word.

As the two aged, they dealt with the disappointments of losing their physical strength and mental faculties. Then they saw the things they had most lived for—their house, their friends, their traveling days, their health—gradually dissipate and vanish. Friends passed away, and the house was sold and traded in for a spot in a retirement community. The travelling needed to cease once their health weakened. The dream was no more and they were left simply with each other's history and love, holding each other by the hand while their world as they knew it became something of the past.

Sadly, their history and their love were not enough to keep them happy and solid. My grandmother was always a talker, and she was hysterically funny. My mother used to tell us how she would play with her dentures

158

at the dinner table, saying tongue-twisters while moving the apparatuses in and out of place. "It was a scream!" she said.

But when her health began to wane, and her eyesight left her—she had macular degeneration—she no longer had the energy to be chatty and hilarious and concerned for others. Her good qualities could no longer compensate for her anger and fears. Unfortunately, it seemed like the anger and the fears were what was left by the time her body failed her and her exterior life held no more entertainment for her. "When I meet God in heaven, I'll have a few things to say to him," she would regally declare. People would always stare blankly at her when she said that because we were all thinking the same thing: God probably wanted a few words with her, too.

When the time came to ensure more intensive care—my granddad was so old, so tired, incapable of caring for my blind grandmother any longer—I went down and found him in a fatigued, withered state. I was deeply, profoundly sad. Sad that his last years were spent in a state of non-peace, sad that he wasn't happier in his marriage, wasn't happier with himself for having done the best he could with impossible circumstances, sad that he couldn't see, as the rest of us could see, that he was a good man. He was weakened when I last saw him, but still the ever-sweet, ever-sensitive soul he had become in his later years.

He wasn't always so gentle. He ran a hardware store in town his whole life and cherished hard work perhaps more than anything else. His childhood was hard, and he had been hardened because of it. But it was remarked at his memorial service (held after we returned from Europe) that he was the living proof that one not need be defined nor imprisoned by a difficult past. He rose above it and raised a family in strength and stability, albeit perhaps not in gentleness. Softness came later. He cried often, laughed more, and held his grandchildren in his wrinkled, softened hands. And he made an effort to be sweet with his wife, which was more than a lot of people could muster.

In his last months, he had suffered a series of strokes and there could no longer be any form of independent living possible for him. So we packed up all their household possessions and put him in a home. I mourned him then. I mourned the life that was no more, mourned the loss of his faculties, mourned the disappointments of his last years, and prayed for God's grace to come and end my life before I would ever get to his state.

On my last night in Pennsylvania, I snuck into his room, and opened up my bag. I pulled out a can of Heineken, two plastic cups and a bottle opener. My Granddad laughed, slowly (everything was slow) and through his calculated breathing said (slowly), "I don't know if we're allowed." I peeked in the hallway and saw the night nurse busy with someone else. I closed the door. "We'll be fast." I poured out the beer, and he didn't say a word, just sipped. We drank in silence, in secret communion, in acknowledgement of the situation he was in, quietly resisting the "no alcohol" rules, all the stupid rules, in fact, and we basked just for a minute in our secret alliance. That's the way I wanted to remember my Granddad.

But cry I did, during that January visit, cry and cry and cry. I packed up every belonging they had, stuffing china and tea towels and knick-knacks into boxes for the auctioneer, listening to my grandmother's wails and complaints that we weren't taking enough items with us. She did all but sneak some pewter trinkets into my suitcase, so much did she want to ensure that they remained in the family. What can I say? They were not destined to become heirlooms. Some things are not destined to be passed on.

So I cried in January. As much as if they had died. And then when I received news that my Granddad actually would die, there weren't as many tears.

The next day I managed to reach someone at home. My father answered the phone and sounded drained, worn out. He told me my grandfather was still alive, and the doctors were not sure whether or not he would come out of his coma. Then he asked me whether or not we were in Spain yet. I smiled over the phone. We had already been in Spain nearly four days, his question showing how much distance there was between the real world and mine on the Camino. People back home couldn't be expected to keep up with our every step. They were dealing with sickness and death and problems. We were in another space, another galaxy. My Granddad's condition was colliding with our pilgrimage world—the real world was back home.

A bit more than a week passed. News of his death came with another email. I didn't mind getting it by email. It would have been impossible to get news any other way. His was in some ways a merciful passing, the end of a road well walked, a quiet finish to a sweet existence. In other ways it was a long and languid departure, not without its calluses and blisters and soreness, not without its regrets, sorrow and loneliness. His death, like his life, cannot be summed up in one emotion, nor one story.

When I shed a few tears on the road about the fact that my Granddad was no longer in this world, I was relieved. I wanted to feel the grief. I didn't want the Camino to cut me off so much that I wouldn't grasp the death of a family member.

And a few days after that, I would be lying in a cold bath, relaxing my muscles after a particularly long day. We'd walked 20 miles that day under the scorching sun on a path that had been so walked upon that the dirt was hard, like asphalt. That particular bit of road was like an old tired-out life. Every now and then, there would be a hint of shade offered from a lone tree on some dried-out patch of long grass. Even in its weathered state, the road was beautiful. Not vibrant, not jubilant, just a quiet, worn beauty through faded colors in the pale greenish-brown grass and the faint grey-blue sky, as if the heat had stopped the colors from brightening. This was a road that was aged, wrinkled and yet had a calming presence on its walkers.

I sat in the bath that evening, listening to music. And then I sobbed. I sobbed long and hard and deeply, feeling the pain of losing my Granddad as my muscles slowly released their tension in the cool water. Nicolas had gone to the bar downstairs. I was alone. And I had just been walking for a very long time.

Granddad

Chapter 24
Day 40

I imagined something serenely spiritual about my fortieth day of pilgrimage, as if I would be joining the ranks of heroes of biblical proportions. Jesus, Moses and others all spent up to forty days in a separate space such as a desert. I just naturally assumed that once I had reached forty days on the Way I would have attained a sort of higher inner status and I would be able to say things like, "Oh, yes, you know you really haven't lived a spiritual journey of discipline until you've done it for forty days. For instance, when I was on the Camino ..."

My Day 40, however, was the most unholy of days except for the fact that we'd entered the Rioja region, a wine county. We were walking from Los Arcos to Logrono, where the scenery changes quite a bit. The landscapes are stunning: fields of wheat against mountains of cedar trees, yards full of olive trees, and everything is still sweet-smelling with paths lined with lavender, thyme, eucalyptus trees, honeysuckle, buttercups and chamomile. It's like being in one great big tea store. But today, neither Day 40 of my walk nor the sweet smells and moments of beauty could save me from myself.

That morning, I had a sore back, achy tendons, suddenly a very heavy bag. (How did that happen?!? Who put a brick in my bag?) And I counted 37 bedbug bites that had reared their ugly heads.

Day 40

A word about bedbugs.

The French fear bedbugs more than death itself. They will drive their cars down tiny village streets barely two meters wide at the speed of lightning, scraping the sides of buildings, leaving tire marks and shouting "Putain!" ("You whore!") at the tops of their lungs as if it were no more risky than a stroll in the park. But show them a dreaded *Cimux lectularius* (the medical term for bedbug in case you were wondering) and they'll shudder in fear, running in the opposite direction crying for their mothers, "J'ai horreur ! J'ai horreur!" ("What a horror!")

This is why when we arrived at various monasteries in France we would have to leave our shoes at the door, and our packs would have to be transported in huge plastic bags treated with bug spray. The beds all had protective covers; volunteers regularly checked the rooms for signs of the little critters (hint: look for tiny brown and red streaks on the mattresses). As soon as there was the merest detection of an infestation, "radio bedbug" would jump into action. This would entail a phone call between lodgings at different villages, so that if one place ever found the bugs, the next stop on the road could give the walkers a warm Camino welcome, complete with surgical gloves, disinfectant and pitchforks.

The Spanish, however, have a much more *carpe diem* approach to the problem, as if to say, "Si, they exist ... but first let's go eat some tapas." As far as I could see there were no bedbug sprays available at the inns or hostels, no warning signs on the walls listing the fates of those bitten. Really, it's like the Spanish are simply determined to prove that they can take on the miseries of the trail with a much cheerier disposition than the French.

So, back to my 37 bites. There are a gamut of emotions that one experiences on the Camino. The ones associated with the discovery of 37 bedbug bites range between disgust and panic to vibrant bitterness that my partner got NOT A ONE.

"Lemme see your legs again," I say to Nic.

He hoists up his foot. "There are no bites on me!" he sings to the "Pinnochio" tune. "Aargh! I don't get it!" I wail.

"I guess I'm just a more careful peregrino than you, Jen. Didn't you take a nap on the mattress?"

"Hogwash. You're not more careful, you're just more lucky. People get bitten all the time when they're sleeping right in their sleeping bags."

Ann, the Canadian walker we'd met in Pamplona, walks over and checks out my legs. "You know," she says kindly, "I feel that the bedbug episode is a true part of the pilgrim experience. Personally, I'll be disappointed if I end my pilgrimage without a single bedbug bite."

"Honey, that is the nicest thing anyone's said to me all day," I reply, shooting a look Nicolas' way. Ann wishes me luck and tells me she'll meet up with us in Logrono, our day's destination.

As I was in the midst of contemplating the fact that my legs had served as a buffet to the insects of the night, Jean-Claude, a middle-aged, somewhat adolescent cyclist pilgrim from France, rode right up next to us. He took one look at my legs and shook his head. People react differently to being bitten, he explained, examining my ever-reddening pocks and welts. Some people get bitten and it never even shows.

"I, however, am like you," he comments. "I react quite badly to bites. I do believe the only solution is for us to stay in the same bedroom." And then he howls in laughter and winks at Nicolas. He takes another look at my arms.

"Yes, yes ... they can be quite ferocious, les petites punaises ... Sometimes," he lowers his voice, "they get to town on, you know, more intimate parts ... has this been the case with you?" he asks, a look of fearful concern on his face.

"No," I say, looking at him squarely, hoping that's the end of the interrogation. Discussing lady problems with a middle-aged man in spandex shorts is frankly not on my list of desired Camino experiences.

"Ah, well, that's good," he says, seemingly relieved. Because, you know, the real tragedy of all this would be for the woman 30 years his junior to have bites on her private parts. Because then she'd really be damaged goods.

"Well, my dear, there's but one solution," he concludes. "You need to go to the pharmacy. Get a professional to look at it. You'll probably need a medicated cream, from the look of those bites."

I look back to my legs and gasp. They are now mutating. Red, swollen and burning. I turn to Nic, my face obviously twisted in horror. He takes me by the hand, "Come on, my lovely leper. Let's get you to a drug store."

Thus, we face the next challenge in Spain. I am slowly learning some of the basic phrases in Spanish (I'd like to reserve a room, one coffee please ...) but the one I seem to be using the most is "No abierto?" meaning, "Not open?" I have been in Spain for seven days and have yet to stumble upon a post office that is open. "No abierto!"

Everything, and I mean everything, is closed before 8 a.m., during siesta from 2 to 5 p.m. (or in certain villages, 3 to 6 p.m., and in others 1 to 4 p.m.). The one exception seems to be the cafe bars. You can apparently close a clinic, a church, a grocery store and a hotel, but never can one deny a Spaniard's access to coffee or alcohol.

Also, there are closures on holy days of which there are a significant number. Ascension Monday, anyone? How about Trinity Fiesta? Those were just this week, not to mention Sundays. And today, bedbug day happens to be a Sunday.

Farmacia on a domingo? No Abierto!

The schedule is frankly counter-productive for the majority of pilgrims, who get up at the crack of dawn to beat the sun (before anything is open), usually arrive at their destination around 2 or 3 in the afternoon (right around siesta), and get to bed between 9 or 10 at night (when most Spaniards are having their supper).

"Honestly," I fume to Nicolas in my state of cultural insensitivity, "What do they DO during the day? Don't they ever WORK?" Something of a misplaced question in a country where unemployment had just hit 22 percent, insinuating that perhaps, no, they actually don't work. Ouch.

We eventually arrive in Logrono. The last bit of walking is through a suburban area, and the sweetness of the vineyards and olive trees are long gone. Asphalt sidewalks and open industrial streets scorch us from the soles of our feet upwards and the beating sun brings the temperature up to about 104 degrees Fahrenheit. Walkers are dragging themselves into the monastery, sunburnt and dehydrated.

To my relief I see Célia, and fish out some pity from her as I mournfully recount my day. Célia, true to her French tradition, shudders, "J'ai horreur!" and takes my bag and promptly puts everything in the wash. She hands me a spray she brought from France.

"On your sleeping bag and in your backpack," she orders. Then she peers at my face, and asks maternally, "Are you feeling all right?" I shake my head, feeling sort of faint.

"Go lie down," Célia says with kind sternness. "You probably took in too much sun."

I follow suit. This day sucks.

I'm about to go crash when I hear a familiar voice: "Chica!"

I turn around. "Natalie!" Natalie and Mia squeal.

"I thought I'd never see you again!"

Natalie rolls her eyes. "Do you know how many people say that to us?"

I wince, "Sorry. When did you get in?"

She looks bashful. "We took the bus. And we're staying at the hotel around the corner. Don't judge! My knee gave out, couldn't go on."

I hold up my hands in innocence, "No judgment. Look at what happened to me." The two of them gasp, coo and caw, pull out anti-itch cream, and tell me they're taking everyone out for drinks and tapas.

"OK!" My spirits lift " Let me go get Nic."

"See?" Nic says to me a little while later, "your bad day becomes good with just some nice company and the appearance of an American Express card."

Back to my bites. The next morning, many bites are still large and omnipresent, but thankfully, without the presence of new ones, I have but one objective: find a pharmacy.

We walk for about an hour and then come upon a town that looks promising. I tentatively give a little push to a pharmacy door, daring to hope. It opens. "Es abierto?" I cry in joy. The two pharmacists, obviously enthralled that someone could be so happy at just the mere fact of being able to set foot within their shop, immediately join me in my enthusiasm, "Abierto? SÌ!! Buenos Dias, signora!! SÌ!!"

"I feel like I've gone to Disneyland!" I whisper to Nic.

"OK, honey."

Now for the language part. I have no idea how to say bedbugs in Spanish, so I simply show them my legs. "Oooo, bzzz?" one asks.

"Sì, en la cama!" I reply, suddenly remembering the word for bed.

"La cama? Ooo, sì, chinches!"

"Chinches!" Nic and I both repeat.

The pharmacists smile, looking pleased at themselves. Mystery solved.

"So where you from?" asks one, presuming I no longer had any more questions on the subject of the bites.

"Montreal."

His face lights up, "Montréal? Aaah," his eyes turn upwards and he puts his hands together as if to pray, "San Joseph. Beautiful Oratory."

"Sì," I nod, "San Joseph. Did you see anything else?"

"No, no times. Had to go to Toronto. See the CN Tower."

Of course. Because if you're Spanish and only have time to see one thing in Montreal, it's Saint Joseph's Oratory. Because there aren't enough churches in Spain.

"So getting back to my bites ... I need a spray for my bag."

"Ah, sì, a spray-aerosol ..."

"Sì."

"There exists no such thing."

"What?" I look at Nic in despair. "But I need a spray! You know, once of those cans with a little skeleton head on the bottle, preferably. Something toxic that will probably give me cancer in twenty years, maybe destroy the ozone a bit? I would trust that sort of thing to kill the eggs!"

The pharmacist looks me pityingly. "No, no ... no aerosol. Wash things in hot water ... muy caliente. I give you cream."

He then explains in a mix of French, English and Spanish that my bites reacted badly in the sun, which is why they were so ugly, and so, if possible, drink water and stay in the shade. I look at him blankly, wanting to say something sarcastic, but he has such a sweet, helpful look on his face that I hold back. I take the cream, thanking him.

We stop in a square, and, completely throwing modesty out the window, I pull up my shirt to just under my bra and begin rubbing on the cream.

"You know," I say to Nic. "Had this happened at home, being covered in bites, dealing with sun reactions and feeling generally horrible, I definitely would have called in sick and taken a day off."

Day 40

Nic looks up at me. "True that. Ready to keep walking?" he asks.

"Yup. Let's go. I'm good for another 14 miles."

Chapter 25
Choices

On Day 42, we walked for hours and hours through dark green woods, which are part of the tip of the Sistema Iberico mountain range. For some reason, it was an incredibly quiet day, with few walkers on the road. Many of our walking mates—Mia, Natalie, Célia and Ann—have decided to stay in Granon. We decided to walk further, all the way to San Juan de Ortega. Every now and then a cyclist would whiz past us on the gravel path, leaving us behind in his dust for us walking, walking, walking again alone.

There was so much sun that day and yet it was quite dark and cool on that lonely path of forest. We sauntered over a small hill, sometime after lunch, and, as if on a cloud, the monastery appeared through the trees. We walked down the road and arrived in town.

Well. Town is an overstatement. It's a large church and monastery, open that day for pilgrims, and then three farm houses that no doubt used to belong to the handful of families who worked for the monks. There is one small hotel for those of us desiring just a hint of luxury and one café, both run by the same pair of brothers. Most pilgrims stay in the monastery.

We had arrived at the beginning of the afternoon and the sun was bright. Out from the shade of the trees, the grounds are exposed to a light that is almost blinding. There are a good many cyclists who stop here for the night, and some of them camp on San Juan's front yard. The church is so big and the people are so few, that the town sort of mellows down into a meditative quietness. A sort of humming sound installed itself, created from the air, the trees and the heat, so that even if most people are not in prayer or contemplation, time and space stand still. The afternoon seemed to go on forever. It stretched out under the sun. There was nothing to do, but I am not bored. I am still.

"I'm not tired," says Nic.

"That's good," I reply. "We did walk quite a bit."

"No, I mean, my mind is not tired. I don't feel weighed down by the burdens of life. I think it's because I don't have any decisions to make."

"What do you mean?"

"Every morning back home I need to decide what outfit to wear. And then I need to decide what to eat. Do I make a pot of coffee before leaving for work or do I stop on the road and buy a cup? Should I fill up the gas tank to the full or the half? From the minute I get up to the moment I lie down at night, my life is filled with decision-making, every step of the way. Here, it's not, not really. Get up, get dressed (only one outfit, so nothing to choose from), eat the food in front of you, and walk on the path laid out before you."

"You know," I say, "sometimes it's not just a matter of making decisions. Sometimes what's exhausting is having so much choice. I think society, or at least consumerism, wants us to believe that having a lot of choice is the ultimate freedom. But you and I have had seemingly little choice here, and we feel lighter, liberated."

"That's what I mean!" cries Nic. "For supper, we have one restaurant where we can go. And supper starts at 7:00, not before, not after. There's not even a Tienda (a general store) here. We don't even have the choice to cook for ourselves. And on the menu there are only three possible meals we can order. So, a no-brainer. Literally. We have no great decisions to make about where to eat, what to eat and what time. And you know what? My mind is cleared, cleaned, free. I'm not bogged down."

Was Nicolas onto something? In North America, we seek comfort, convenience and consumer's choices more than any other place on earth. I am often surprised, every time I am in Europe, especially in rural areas, at the relatively small size of their stores, even the necessary ones, such as pharmacies or the grocer's. I have also noticed comparatively fewer malls, and fewer stores of the same type within walking distance of each other.

The city is very guilty of this phenomenon. I think about Ste-Catherine's street, our main commercial strip in downtown Montreal. My theory is that there's actually the same, in essence, nine stores that are just duplicated over and over in a three-mile distance. You have the women's professional clothing, the men's professional clothing, the urban trendy clothing, a bookstore, a gadget store, the Apple store, the wine and liquor store, a shoe store and a movie theatre. Over and over and over, covering the entire downtown. And that doesn't even cover our four or five malls and department stores, included in the same distance.

This time in Europe, being in such rural areas and crossing such small towns, the difference is even more striking between their consumer lifestyle and ours. One fruit store, in the centre of town. One butcher. One pharmacy, the size of which could fit into the ladies' hygiene aisle of a North American pharmacy. Maybe the inhabitants of these towns would appreciate a bit more choice, or at least a bit more competition between distributers, because it would no doubt bring the prices of their products down. I asked a friend of mine who studies economics about this, and she told me that the debate is called the illusion of choice.

"Modern capitalism is based on the fundamental principle that freedom is better for the individual and that more choice expands one's freedom. The problem is that when we get into those small communities, those tiny villages, if you open a second pharmacy, you'll no doubt hurt the first one. There's not enough market for two. Consumers may get lower prices for a time, but the prices will necessarily go back up once one of the two competitors closes, and all you've succeeded in doing is shutting down a small business."

The illusion of choice. It's true on so many levels. Barry Schwartz's book, *The Paradox of Choice*, states that too much choice actually increases paralysis in the consumer (when there's too much to choose from, you will end up not making any decision at all) and decreases happiness (when you have too much choice, your expectations in the end result are too high.)

In all these little rural towns, we always had exactly what we needed, despite the lack of choice, despite the ridiculous Spanish opening hours, despite our lack of bag space. Not once, not even during the bedbug crisis, the heat waves of the first week in Spain, or during my unhappy feminine week of the month, was I up the creek without a pharmaceutical paddle, not in a really dire sense. To be sure, we were vigilant, well-planned and well-packed. But we also realized that we were not in need of a 24-hour Wal-Mart at every corner. You just don't need that much availability of choice.

Spiritually speaking, when you clear your mind of clutter, you clear it of burden. These Camino days, I am not weighed down by having to choose from sixty different brands of washing detergent. Nor am I distracted by dozens of clothing stores that basically sell me the same thing, trying to convince me that theirs are the items I cannot live without. When your mind has been de-cluttered, you can begin to go places you didn't even know existed. This must be very scary for many people. It was just new for me.

San Juan de Ortega is neither the prettiest place we visited, nor the most culturally vibrant. It didn't have the best food, the best party nor the most meaningful encounters. But it had something much, much better: emptiness, vast space both physically and spiritually, and a total lack of choice.

We sat for hours, taking in the air and the sun, gazing at cream-tinted stones. We went to Mass and didn't understand the priest, but didn't need to, either. We ate supper in the bar with Marta, a German-American woman who we met that day, and we chatted about everything and anything, and nothing of real consequence. I was grateful to meet this new person. We discovered Morcillos de Burgos—

fried blood pudding, which is a Spanish delicacy—and then we sat some more. Doing simply nothing.

Choices

Chapter 26
Ian

I have just met the most annoying man alive and he is sleeping two doors down from me. Also, to my utter embarrassment, he's Canadian. From Toronto. When a fellow walker is rude, negative, clingy, homophobic, slightly racist and the worst kind of conservative right-wing Christian, you want them at least to not be of the same nationality as you. You want them, say, to come from Texas. Incidentally, there are three Texans on the road these days. They are absolutely the sweetest, most equable people I have ever met. Damn. And even the sweet Texans have a hard time shouldering this man.

Ian joined up with our division right during the Pyrenees and quickly developed a reputation for himself as being one of the worst Camino mates around. Typically, he would trail us for hours on end, complaining the whole time about the Spaniards, the food, the loudness on the road, the *hospitaleros* last night, that time he was in France and all alone, ending each sentence in "It was awful, just awful. This is my last Camino!" His latest complaint is that priests in Spain won't hear confession in English. Never mind that we're, you know, in Spain, never mind that he doesn't speak Spanish, never mind that you'd be hard pressed to find a small town Canadian priest who would take confession in any language other than his own, this latest issue bothers Ian to no end. Despite his intolerable presence, my skewered curiosity of the man haunts me so that I will not shake him.

177

For one thing, he makes for terrific gossip.

By day three of his presence on the road, the normally friendly-natured, peace-seeking pilgrims begin to crack and we start sharing stories, ranting about the latest debacles brought forth by the infamous Ian.

"So this morning," begins Ann, our fellow Canadian friend, "I am sipping my coffee and in comes Ian. He starts telling me about the last time he was in Madrid and how he absolutely had to get out of that God-forsaken town because it was gay-pride weekend and he couldn't stand the sight of it. 'It was awful, just awful.' So, Ian, I tell him, what is your problem with gays?"

"You shouldn't have opened that can of worms with him." I tell her.

"Don't I know it! What a mistake. He chews my ear off for the next 45 minutes about how wrong homosexuality is, those asshole liberal churches who allow gay marriage, all that the Bible has to say on the matter ... I finally just grabbed my poles and said. 'Look at the time' to rid myself of him."

"Well, he got us afterwards," Nic says. "First he begins to rail on about the Greek Orthodox because their pilgrimage to Mount Athos is so complicated and exclusive. Then he makes some comment about how at least with the Catholics and Orthodox still don't allow for gay marriage. Then he turns to Jenna and says, only half joking, 'I'm going back to Mount Athos. NO WOMEN ALLOWED.'"

"To his credit, he's right. There are no women allowed on Mount Athos," I pitch in.

"You don't say," replies Ann.

"But then he followed that with ..." as I gesture to Nicolas dramatically ...

"'We'll go to Mount Athos, and you can stay at the bottom and do our laundry,'" Nicolas mimics Ian's nasal voice.

Ann throws her head back and laughs. "Oh no! He was joking, of course."

"Yes, but in the space of one conversation, he'd managed to insult another religion, gays, and women. I should have told him my uncle is Russian Orthodox and gay," says Nic.

"Who used to be a woman, just to complete the whole thing," I offer.

"That would have done it," agrees Ann.

It appears, however, that not much "will do it" with Ian. The poor fellow is incapable of taking a hint.

"I'm waiting for Charles and his two stooges," says Ian to us one night from the plaza, referring to a trio of French students who are doing a two-week trek on the Camino.

"Do they know you're here?" I ask.

"Oh, yeah, I told them. Those three are so broke, they've been living off bread and granola for the past four days. I told them, 'Listen, meet me at the plaza, and I'll pay for your dinner on my credit card. No big deal.' They said they'd think about it. I think they feel shy about taking charity."

"Shy about charity might be the least of their feelings right now," mutters Nicolas, as I elbow him. In dear Charles' and his two stooges' defense, Ian had been trailing them for the past three days and they simply couldn't shake him. It seemed no matter what inn they were booked at, no matter where they stopped for a rest, there would be Ian booming out, "Well, HELLO! I wondered where you'd gone off to. You won't believe what just happened to me. It was awful, just awful."

"Well, Ian, if we see them, we'll send them your way," I say politely, thinking to myself that it would be more of a warning than an invitation.

"It's so sad," says Nic as we walk away.

"What is?"

"He's so lonely. All he's looking for these days is some company."

"Do you think that's why he keeps on doing Caminos?" I ask, thinking about Ian's revelation to me this morning that this was in fact his fourth time walking the Saint James Way.

"Probably. He's trying to get something here he probably can't get at home. Everyone at home has no doubt dumped him."

I look back at him wistfully. We're only one stop from Burgos by now and everyone is in major social mood. It's always that way when we reach an urban setting. The solitude of the road is on hold while all the *peregrinos* party and hit the town, drinking wine and eating tapas, moving in clusters and cliques and groups with their newfound Camino buddies. Only Ian sits alone on a bench in the plaza, waiting for his mates to find him.

"Should we go back and offer to eat with him?" I ask Nicolas.

"No, Jen. You'll just get frustrated and so will I. Spending time with Ian is more than an act of charity. It requires the patience of a Zen monk. Or a deaf ear."

We head out the next day. Célia tells us that Charles and his two mates got up at the crack of dawn and took the bus ahead a town or two just to make sure they would be far enough from a certain someone. Célia is the image of discretion and kindness and would never dream of saying anything cruel, even of the most unseemly of people.

We stop at a cafe and who do we meet? Ian.

"My best friend gave me my poles," he says, motioning towards his walking sticks.

"Who's your best friend?"

"He's Father Mark. Our parish priest. He's the one who gave me the idea of going on my first Camino."

"Oh, really?"

"Yeah, he said it's good for people's spiritual development to do a pilgrimage. I've told him this one's my last, though. No more Caminos for me."

"Hmm."

"Then he told me about the Camino del norte, which is where I went on my second pilgrimage."

"Again his idea?"

"Of course. He's very well informed about the Camino. He says he can't do them because of his commitments at church, but he's just happy that I get to do the walks. He's the one who pays my way."

I nearly choke on my cafe con leche. "Your priest friend funds your trips?"

"Yeah, every one. Priests don't need a whole lot to live on. So he's pretty generous with his money."

"And extremely creative on ways to get some Ian-free time," whispers Nicolas behind me.

"Well," I say, stunned. "How about that."

Nicolas and I say goodbye to Ian and head back on the trail.

"May it never be said that intelligent, innovative priests don't exist. Father Mark is the living proof that they do."

"Here's to Father Mark," says Nic, raising his water bottle.

And here's the thing about broken souls on a pilgrimage. Loneliness can be a terrible thing, and you are not safe from it on the Camino. Walking several hours a day will not heal loneliness, bad social skills, addiction or any other affliction we may be trying to rid ourselves of.

Sleeping in a dormitory won't fix your obsessive-compulsive disorder. Making a bunch of pilgrim friends won't heal your low self-esteem. Living temporarily without the luxuries of a middle-class, yuppy urban lifestyle won't make you less selfish, and turning off technology won't rid you of your stress levels.

Going on a pilgrimage can reveal things about you: your need for control, for instance, or for distraction. It can be a vessel towards healing and transformation. But if you are unaware, or unwilling to address these demons in your closet, the Camino is nothing more than a therapy session in which the patient addresses every statement with, "Yes, but ..."

I learned this through Ian, but I learned it about myself as well, when three months after my return I was going crazy with appointments, deadlines and problems with finances at the center. I was crying at my desk, and a phrase popped into my head, "Jenna, you must find your Camino again." Doing a 65-day walk could not, would not, save me or protect me from my troubles. But it could help me understand, and maybe meet those troubles with a bit more maturity. It could provide me with the memory of certain lessons so that when my problems reared their ugly heads and they would, believe me— I would at least be better equipped with certain thoughts and certain realizations that I had acquired along the way.

Ian would not, could not, be saved from his loneliness, simply because he kept on going for long walks and meeting new passels of people once the last passel had ditched him. I get it. He was searching to fill some void. But the painful truth is that if people found him obnoxious on the trail, they probably found him obnoxious at home as well. And that is the very thing that he could not escape from, no matter how many miles he put under his feet.

It wasn't for lack of trying, however. A year later I received an email from Ann. She'd decided to do another Santiago pilgrimage, this time starting in Portugal. She wrote, "Sitting in an Internet cafe in Porto, full of pilgrims on their way to Santiago. GUESS WHO JUST WALKED IN?"

Chapter 27
Burgos

The days are hot. By noon I can feel my skin's pores gulping and gasping for air. I talk to Michelle, a thirtysomething woman who has been walking for as long as we have, having started in France through the chemin de Vezelay. "I feel like I have just begun my walking!" she cries frustratedly. "I can't find my rhythm ..." I tell her it was the same for us. "The heat just wears you down so much."

"We've got to start getting up earlier and leaving faster," Nicolas says one morning and I groan. I say to him, "I can't move faster in the morning. I already feel like we're on an army march."

Nicolas and I are still having a hard time with each other's pace. Sometimes he's so far ahead of me, he'll actually stop and sit down for a granola bar while I catch up.

"Just try it," he urges me. "Think about it—arriving at our destination right after noon. You can skip the day's heat."

So that's what we begin to do. Nic sets his alarm for a little before six and we get up as quietly as possible, hoping not to disturb our roommates. We are on the road by 6:30. The sun is sometimes not quite up, but the air is already warm. There is a quietude to these mornings. The experienced walkers tell us the Camino is quiet this year, perhaps because of the poor economy in Spain. We are often alone on the road at this hour, or with just the odd person here or there. Our morning rituals become sacred for me. We walk for three or four miles which usually brings us into our first town of the day. By this time, cafes are opening. It's time for breakfast. Our second breakfast, that is. We usually have some fruit and a granola bar right when we leave, enough to tie us over until the cafe. Pilgriming puts you on something of a hobbit's diet.

At the cafe, it's the usual, cafe con leche, a latte of sorts. But these ones are sweeter, creamier, thicker than the ones at home. Then we order a tortilla con patata, which is like a thick omelet stuffed with potatoes. You feel heartier after this, and the days of meager French breakfasts are long behind us.

We enter Burgos about two weeks into Spain. Being in a city is fun because you get the rare experience of being able to choose your restaurant and your hotel. Entering a city in Spain is less fun, because the last three miles before the city center are spent walking through suburbs, industrial neighborhoods or along highways. I am a city girl at heart. I love the urban life, the proximity urban living provides to all amenities, the diversity, the beauty of the buildings, bustle and hustle of its streets and events. I find cities beautiful.

When you drive into a city, you can pass quickly through industrial zones or lifeless suburban areas annexed onto the outskirts of a metropolis. When you are walking, these zones stick out like a sore thumb. They are not esthetic, but they can be necessary. A city needs its factories, its outer suburban population, its auto repair sections, and dare I say it, its mega-stores to continue to thrive. In a balanced existence, the urban core and the outer zones mutually feed each other, both in populations and economic activity. You realize that your beautiful downtown, your quaint historical quarters also depend on these industrial, commercial areas for their continued economic well-being, and for the pockets of populations who contribute to the growth of the urban hub, but who live just outside it.

There is so much beauty along the Camino, both in France and in Spain, that the moments of ugliness on display in the outer urban zones really hit you in the face. Concrete sidewalks, mega stores with plastic paneling, chain-linked fences, cookie-cutter houses with double garages, all these things swoop us out of our pilgrim trance and dump us right in the middle of modern-day mayhem. We'd read enough horror stories of the entrance into Burgos that we broke the cardinal rule of the walker and took the bus. Leave the suburbs and the factory district to the purists. We had a Cathedral to see.

And what a cathedral it was. Burgos is basically one big church with a small city built around it. It is epic, magnificent and gigantic, more castle and mega-museum than cathedral. In fact, another way to look at it is that the Cathedral of Burgos was actually at one point a city in itself. It had residences, two cloisters, more chapels than I could count, work spaces, kitchens and stables. People could theoretically live, work, worship and feed themselves without ever stepping outside the exterior walls of the cathedral.

We have supper with our usual cohort—Robert and Célia, who have been preoccupied with mending their war wounds, Natalie and Mia—who caught up to us by taxi—and Ann, who will be flying out tomorrow. Another last supper! Saying goodbye to walking friends becomes as common as meeting new ones.

"How did you like the cathedral?" I ask Ann.

"Beautiful. More of a castle than a church. Personally, though, as far as religious buildings are concerned, nothing comes close to Eunate."

"That's right, I forgot that you stayed there!" I exclaim, feeling a bit of regret. Eunate is a small, octagonal-shaped chapel located a little bit from Puenta La Reina. We visited it during our first week in Spain. I had no idea we could stay there, so Nicolas and I walked on after our visit, but ever since then, pilgrims have told us about the moving and quieting experience they had there. The hosts are typically missionary types from abroad who see their service of hospitality as a vocation. They want the pilgrims to have a contemplative, healing time at the church.

"It was just such a special place," says Ann, a bit dreamily. "We were led into the chapel after supper, and we all sat by candlelight, quietly. Then the host washed our feet. Can you believe that? This is embarrassing, but I began to cry. I think there was just so much that I began feeling at once. I'm not the cry-at-church type."

"What's your religion?" I ask, the same way I would ask, "What's your poison?"

"I was raised Methodist. Now I go to a liberal, Episcopalian church. I enjoy hearing Christians say gay-friendly things."

"I was raised Mennonite. Now I go to a Quaker meeting. I enjoy hearing Christians say nothing at all," I say. I think about this statement I'd just made. Truth was, I was in an adoption process with a small Anglican parish that I'd spoken at a few times. When I say adoption, I mean they were adopting me. The Quaker meeting was an excellent foster home. They were kind, sincere and passionate about wonderful things such as love and the environment. I enjoyed the silent worship most of all. But being at my Anglican parish reminded me I wasn't ready to give up on the sacraments just yet. I may have sworn off church, and certainly spiritual experiences in church, but Jesus and his sacraments do have a trump card with me.

"The thing about it," says Ann, "is I always figured I was past being able to have a spiritual experience, especially in a church. Eunate proved me wrong."

Célia pipes in. "You know," she says, "I talked to a hostess at an inn who was telling me about the supposed energy fields at Eunate. Apparently thousands of years ago there was a river where the chapel stands, and so it symbolizes the meeting of water, land and fire, because it's located on a hot spot where the sun's rays hit it. There's all sorts of theories about its construction. Some think it was the Templars, others, the Saint John's Order of Knights ... no one's sure. It is very old, that's all we know."

"Energy fields!" I exclaim. "Sounds esoteric!"

"My hostess would say it is," replies Célia. "She claimed that chairs could levitate at a certain spot in the church. A guide showed her once. Two people lifted a chair with her sitting on it, with only one finger each. I didn't have the heart to tell her that the guide was playing a trick. If two people hold a chair at the right balance, they can lift it off the ground with just the tips of their fingers, even with someone sitting on it."

I rolled my eyes. "And your hostess believed this?"

"Your story disturbs me," says Ann. "I lived something very real there, something very profound, no magic, no tricks, nothing esoteric. Just quiet peace and acceptance, and ... closeness, although I don't know to what. And now I hear that guides and tourists are using the place to, I don't know, get their science-fiction fix?"

Célia pats her hand. "My dear, I have been a Catholic all my life. I no longer go to church. I have a faith; I am fully capable of saying that. But if I had to sit through one more session with an old aunt telling me to sleep with the picture of Saint Anthony under my pillow for three nights if I wanted to find a husband, I would go mad. People will ALWAYS opt for the magic tricks, even when an encounter with the Spirit of God, like the one you had, is being offered to them at the tips of their fingers."

"An encounter with the Spirit of God," says Ann, reflectively. "An encounter. Huh."

Leaving Burgos in the morning was one of our more miserable experiences. First, at 7 am we had to walk through throngs—and I mean literally masses—of university students and partygoers who were heading home from the night's festivities. The day before had been the holiday of Saint Jean Baptiste. That's the thing about Spanish cities. Their hustle and bustle is on a totally different level compared to France.

"Let me get this right," says Nic to me. "La Fête Saint-Jean is actually Quebec's national holiday, but the Spanish celebrate it harder than we do?"

"Seriously," I agree, trying to avoid broken glass on the ground while looking away from a young twenty-something urinating against a wall, "Their Saint-Jean puts our Saint-Jean to shame." I watch as another hoard of people dance by us, laughing and holding beer bottles. We navigate our way through the city streets, trying to find our Camino markers.

Then we need to walk our way through the suburbs, on sidewalks through cookie cutter streets and along service roads. Complicated to get in, complicated to get out, this city was. Eventually we are in nature.

"La Meseta!" says a Brazilian who passes us by.

"What?"

"La Meseta. Spanish desert. You will have no cover here. Not from the wind, not from the sun. Be careful."

I look ahead. The road goes on and on, stretching out over white rocks, rough trees, wheat and shrubbery. It's dusty.

And hot.

"God almighty, you could fry an egg on the road," I pant to Nic.

I say this as we enter Hornillos del Camino. The town is one street long. In someone's basement you can find the convenience store. There is one church, one bar, one hostel. All you need to become a major stopping point along the Camino. Every night, this town's population of 70 just about doubles with the influx of walkers who stop here and then hemorrhage out early the next morning. Like San Juan de Ortega, the town doesn't have much to offer in terms of partying, but instead of the spiritual stillness of San Juan, this town has a whole lot to offer in terms of oddity.

Hornillos literally translates into "little ovens." Along the paths that lead to peoples' homes are little grottos covered in long, overgrown grass. They are in reality tiny mud huts dug into the ground in dotted fashion along fields, grown over by long grass, making them look like mole hills or hobbit homes. These grottos are actually bread ovens. It seems that this hamlet used to be the bakery for the larger surrounding districts.

They no doubt were the main suppliers of baked goods to all of Burgos for a time. Bread was its lifeline. The grottos sit empty now, or are used as wine cellars or storage. Burgos makes its own bread, or has large industrial suppliers, like the ones we saw coming into town. You can still see tiny pipe chimneys poking through the grass, and when you peek into the ovens, you'll see the stone shelves upon which the loaves used to bake.

The only cool place in town is its large church, the stonewalls thick enough to keep out light and heat.

Hornillos is one of those enigmatic little towns that you feel must be as old as time. And yet is difficult to define. Pilgrim blogs speak mostly of the sketchy overnight experiences spent in the town's gymnasium on occasions when the refugio is full. This thankfully was not our fate.

After we got a bed in the local refugio, we spent the rest of the afternoon lounging about in the church. Marta, the woman we met in San Juan de Ortega, walks in and plops down on the bench beside me.

"Hello!" I exclaim, happy to see a familiar face. I am still mourning Ann's departure.

"The weather was fine up until noon," says Marta, "but now I am finding it rather unlivable!"

"We have been sitting on a church bench for two hours, not daring to move for fear of dehydration, and there is not so much as a convenience store in town," I complain. "Nic, you said if we leave earlier, we can party all afternoon. Where's the party?"

"Mmm ...,"groans Nic, "stop talking, it's too hot."

Marta simply sighs and puts a cold wash cloth on her face. "It's going to be like this for the rest of the week. Hot, hot, hot."

"I'm bored," I say."I miss the city. I need cafes and air conditioning and museums and stores. This small-town-empty-your-mind crap is not working for me anymore."

"Mmm," they both reply.

"Who wants to grab a drink at the cafe?"

"Mmm ...,"groans Marta softly. "It's too hot to move."

I occupy myself by going to the cafe bar and drinking cold beer, feeling grumpy. In the city I'd have a whole plaza of cafes. And streets of shops. And museums to visit. This sparse living is for the birds. But one thing can be said for outer-urban living in Spain. You can, even in the most remote, desolate, boring places along the Camino, count on the availability of beer.

Bottoms up.

Chapter 28
Camino Pains

On the morning we left Hornillos del Camino, somewhere around Day 14 of Spain and Day 46 of our pilgrimage, we bump into our usual crowd at a café about two hours down the road. "Good grief," I say, plopping down on a chair, "you all look like you got into a fight with the road, and the road won!"

Natalie has her bandaged leg propped up on a chair, Mia is popping Advil, and Célia and Robert look as though they could do with about three years' worth of uninterrupted sleep. Natalie groans and looks my way. "Have you noticed that there are some people on this trek who aren't getting so much as a blister? Not a blister."

"Yes," I reply, "those people will not be welcome at my table."

"I sat in the bath yesterday and actually pondered the possibility that the Camino may kill me," says Natalie. "I truly wondered if I would die. My muscles are strained, my knee is swollen, I've had bouts of dehydration and did I mention an allergic reaction to a horse?"

"A horse? Where did you see a horse?"

"Farmland right outside of Burgos. It was actually a dog that ran up to us on the road, and I began playing with it. Damn me and my love of all creatures great and small. Turns out it was a farm dog who'd been hanging out in some stables, and my eyes began swelling to the size of golf balls. A horse, Jenna. I had to go to the clinic and get EpiPened because of a friggin' HORSE!" She throws her head back and groans again "The books don't warn you about the body stuff."

"Especially not about needing an EpiPen in case of encountering a horse-rubbed dog," says Nic.

I nod. The books don't warn you. Mia smiles at me. "You wanna know mom's secret weapon?" She pulls out a ziplock bag stuffed with multicolored pills. Nicolas and I gape and then burst out laughing,

"Holy crap, Natalie! What are you, a pusher?"

"Our mantra," says Mia, "is 'a rest on the crest, a pill on the hill.' We invented it on the first day. At the top of the road, you take a break, on the top of the hill, you pop Advil."

"Laugh all you want," Natalie says calmly. "These babies are keeping me a pilgrim. I'll build a shrine to Ibuprofen when I arrive in Santiago. In any case, my horse incident is nothing compared to what Célia's been through these past two days."

I peer over to Célia and realize she was looking very wane. She and Robert had both lost momentum over the past week, lagging behind and needing more rest. Nicolas and I had talked about it in Burgos, worried mostly about their states of mind. Bodily fatigue was one thing, but Célia's spirits had taken a hit. She hadn't been as cheerful and Robert was dragging his feet more and more.

"How are you feeling?" I ask her.

"Well, ma chère," she begins, "we left Burgos in the heat of the day and got about four miles out of town when I suddenly felt the need to sit down."

"Heat exhaustion?"

"Something like that. I immediately began sweating so profusely that my clothes were drenched, within minutes."

"That's never a good thing."

"Hmm," she agrees. "Of course, the really worrisome episode happened right afterwards, when I urinated blood."

I gasp. "Célia that's awful!"

She nods, "To be frank, I've never felt so afraid in my life. Robert got me on the phone to a doctor and they sent me an ambulance. Spent the night in the hospital in Burgos. It was a slight bladder infection, brought on by dehydration."

"When did you get out?"

"Yesterday morning. We caught up to you pretty well, didn't we?"

I pause. "Célia ... do you mean to tell me that yesterday you walked from Burgos to here, meaning ..." I do a quick calculation, "at your exit from the hospital you walked 18 miles?"

"Yes!" she exclaimed. "I was feeling fine once I was treated. Look at me. A retired woman getting over a stint in the hospital and still on the Camino. Robert, are you ready?"

Poor Robert looks over at me, shrugs his shoulders and together they exit the café.

I look back at the rest of the group. "Did you just see what I saw? Pure insanity? The death wish on two legs?"

Natalie shrugs. "They look OK. And Célia seems really motivated."

"These are relatively normal people who led pretty balanced lives in the real world," I say with wonder. "Put us for a month or two on the Camino and we all become nuts."

"So," says Natalie popping an anti-inflammatory and hoisting herself off the chair, "does this next place have baths?"

"I don't think so," says Nicolas, "it's San Anton."

Chapter 29
San Anton

I am sitting in ruins. To say this makes me incredibly happy. I've been looking forward to the ruins of San Anton ever since Chantal, back in France, told us about them. The weather is still scorching hot. It's around 1 p.m., and we need shade desperately. This works out fine on the day that we arrive at the ruined monastery, because it only took us 10 miles to get there from Hornillos.

San Anton, or Saint Anthony the Abbott as we know him, was the patron saint of a French order of medicinal monks whose specialty was treating a flesh-eating disease common throughout the Middle Ages, sometimes referred to as Saint Anthony's Fire. Turns out the disease was caused by a fungus that grew on wheat. Taking into account how much bread pilgrims ate on a typical day, they were far more susceptible to getting this flesh-eating disease. Therefore San Anton and its monastery became a popular stopping place on the Camino beginning in the year 1146.

In the 16th century, however, the cause of the disease was discovered and the wheat was properly treated   as a result, thus eliminating the disease and the raison d'être for Saint Anthony Order. This also conveniently occurred at a time when Spain and France were at great odds, so the king of Spain   seized the occasion to disband the monks and send the French ones home.

The Monastery was gradually abandoned and the surrounding peasants used the land, both around and in the monastery for their animals and crops. Wintertime on the Meseta took care of the rest and now we have only the supporting walls, a few beautiful arches and the altar space left of the original majestic church. The ground is covered in rock, and in every crumbling alcove the hosts have placed candles. What can I say? A fixer upper has never looked so good.

A family designated by the diocese to take care of the ruins had renovated three rooms. Generally, there is a second family who act as hosts. There is a common room, where we eat, a dormitory for twelve pilgrims, and a washroom void of hot water and electricity. Tonight will be the closest thing to camping during our whole pilgrimage, but it will be one of the more memorable experiences as well.

The family who cares for the monastery's grounds lives and breathes the Camino di Santiago. The mother, a beautiful, dark Spaniard speaks several languages fluently, which allows her to interact with the walkers as they stroll onto the grounds for a rest. They have three young children: Santiago, Juan de Ortega and Theresa, the baby. Do you think they're Catholic? What could possibly have given you that idea?

The father comes and gets us from our siesta and tells us to come and eat. "Es Domingo," he says. It's Sunday. On Sunday, people share meals together. He pulls out a huge paella pan and begins chopping vegetables and washing clams and fish. We watch him fry up the food and then we all cram around a table, a whole lot of ragged, haggard-looking *peregrinos* with two parcels of kids, both the host's and the caretaker's, and we all dive in. Afterwards I go back out to the courtyard and sit on a stone.

There is nothing to do but be. Time is so different here. At home, I am a master list-maker. My day is divided up into fifteen-minute slices. If I take too long a lunch break, I feel guilty. Sometimes I am literally running from one meeting to another. I learned only recently to control how many appointments I would cram in each day. Two is manageable. Three is pushing it, and to be avoided. Four means we are approaching a holiday season or a vacation period. People rush madly around, finishing reports, returning phone calls, getting checks signed and going to one last meeting. What the non-profit world lacks in human resources we make up for in committees.

In San Anton, I will spend eight hours doing nearly nothing. Time is elastic—what passes by so quickly in the real world feels like forever over here. I sit for an hour or two on a bench, sometimes reading, sometimes writing, sometimes not. I am not bored, but my mind drifts from one topic to the next, floating around images, things I read in books, conversations I have had lately.

Time. We don't have enough of it and when we have too much, we don't use it well. Or do we? Is what I am doing right now a waste of time? And who decides what a waste of time really is? Here, there is nothing to absorb time like a vacuum, the way there is back home. No phone, no Internet, no duties. Back home I remember surviving a busy period and thinking it made me feel old. I have less of a concept of age here. I don't feel youngish anymore, the way I did when I was 17, but I certainly don't feel old. The aging process slows down when time expands.

I find it interesting that we are sitting around in a place that was once designated to heal illness and disease. In Medieval Europe, people had to worry about plagues and flesh-eating conditions and they came to the church of their patron saint for healing. In modern-day Western civilization, we don't worry about the same diseases as our ancestors did. But we do worry about time and busyness. Maybe this is our new disease. People are burning out, suffering from anxiety, complaining about life flying by. We go on pilgrimages to slow down, to get away from it all. We have our own set of sicknesses and so we sleep in the remnants of old hospitals, hoping for restoration from this new condition, just as people slept here four or five hundred years ago, hoping for restoration from theirs.

Nicolas comes and sits next to me. He shakes his head. "It doesn't make sense," he says, " It feels like we're sitting in the ruins of Rome, but this monastery was only abandoned 300 years ago. How could it have fallen apart so horribly? There must have been some natural disaster or something. "

Marta overhears him and comes over to us. "It's just what happens when you don't take care of the building. No earthquake, no great storm is necessary. The *hospitalero* told me that once the roof caved in, the local peasants came and took the stones for their houses.

"Still, you'd think a building like this would last," he comments.

"Well," says Marta pensively, "that's what time does, I guess."

Chapter 30
La Meseta

"If there's one part of the Camino that you skip, it's the meseta."

This seems to be the general consensus of opinion.La meseta is an inner plateau, a valley of sorts bordered by mountains on both sides. It starts around Burgos, which for us was the second week of walking in Spain, and you don't really feel its end until Leon, some eight days later.

The first day we entered it, I felt certain that it was desert land. It turns out flatland is a more appropriate term. The road stretches out as far as the eye can see through arid, windblown, sand-colored plains. It would seem that everything grows brown and beige here, never knowing the green of birth. Grass grows beige, plants grow beige, wheat and bushes and herbs grow beige. It is earthy here, dusty and stark. Houses stand two stories high, made of a compound of straw, mud and construction clays, contrasted with bright blue doors and shutters. We see more "hornillos" everywhere, just like in Hornillos del Camino. The donkeys fade into the background, their light chestnut fur matching the shades of the land.

I loved the meseta. I spoke with a fair number of peregrinos who bemoaned its existence, nostalgic for the days of the Pyrenees or the lush hills of Najéra. This was not the case for me.

I remember Canadian author and storyteller Stuart McLean, who once said that most people whine about the boring plainness of the Saskatchewan wheat fields, preferring the "majesty" of the Rockies. Stuart guffaws at this statement. "Who says for something to be beautiful it has to be majestic? Beauty has nothing to do with majesty. Something flat and colorless can be beautiful. I'll take the wheat fields any day."

Well, Stuart, I'll take the Meseta any day. The flat road dipping in and out of shades of red and rust calms the mind. There are no distractions, no noise. When you do come upon a creek, or a tree in bloom, it so takes you by surprise that you don't hesitate, you don't even think, you just drop your bag and sit in the presence of its life. The wind blowing across the plains with only scatterings of trees and shrubs made me feel like I was truly on a pilgrimage.

The weather is the biggest challenge along the meseta. In the winter, its inhabitants talk of the drastically low temperatures, far below freezing, and the winds, of course, make the outdoors uninhabitable, rendering the lifestyle hermitic and insular. In the summer, the sun scorches down on the backs of walkers, the environment offering little or no shade, and water sources, usually abundant on the Camino Frances, are sometimes four or five hours walking distance one from another.

To say that you need to give special attention to your health is an understatement. On our second day out of Burgos, in San Anton, we left at a particularly early hour in an effort to beat the heat. At 6 a.m., the air was already heavy and warm. We set out on the road, beneath the ruined arches of San Anton's monastery and walked 32 kilometers along the dirt path that stretched over a large hill. You walk for hours along these paths, barely in touch with civilization. It was along one of these roads that we discovered the Calzada Romana.

The Calzada Romana, or Roman Road, is the preferred road of the intuitives and die-hards, often avoided in favor of the much more practical Camino Real. It stretches from Sahagun to Mansilla de las Mulas, the last stop before Leon. The Roman Road, as its name reveals, was built by the Roman army during antiquity. Its dirt and rocky path is virtually uninhabited save for one lonely village, Calzadilla de los

Hermanillos. This village survives on some light farming and hosting the pilgrims. There can't be much more than 200 residents.

Years ago, when the village school of Calzadilla shut down, the town residents turned it into a refugio. Nicolas and I stop here and make a donation, as is the tradition in the refugios. We meet up with about a dozen others pilgrims, all of whom we know, and we calculate as a group that we are the only pilgrims in the entire village tonight. It seems everyone else took the modern Camino Real road. Nic and I explore the village—all four streets—and establish that there may be no school, post office or pharmacy, but that there is a bar (of course!). We sit down for a pint.

"So," says Nic, "Let's play, how do the people live?"

We enjoy playing this game, whenever we're in a place that is so far from our own urban lifestyle. Have the villagers lived here their whole life? How do they view the rest of the world? Where do they do their shopping? How do they make an income?

"It amazes me that in the Western world, in one of the countries of the European Union, that we find ourselves in a village such as this." I shake my head. "The houses are made of straw and mud!"

"Aren't you glad?" asks Nic.

"Aren't I glad what?"

"Aren't you glad that there are still villages like this, where in a developed country you can find yourself in a town where things are sparse and slow and seemingly un-modern? It puts things in perspective. Look at the men."

He nods over at the bar. It's about four in the afternoon and about a dozen men are sitting on stools, sipping beer, chatting at the TV screen where a soccer match takes place.

One thing the meseta has done is introduce me to slow paces. By all accounts, this is a slow-paced scene. It's too hot and too isolated to do anything quickly. We spend the mornings walking and the afternoons sitting around, talking, thinking, musing.

"Do you miss the pace at home?" I ask Nicolas.

"Nope. But that doesn't mean I don't love my work."

I nod, thinking about all I like about my work. But then my mind drifts back to the committees, meetings, and the evenings full of work, deadlines and general craziness. My stomach begins to knot.

"I know I like what a slow-paced life is teaching me, but I don't know how to bring back home the lessons I've learned here," I say mournfully. "I could get so stressed. Here, I work hard, I feel pain, but my mind is clear. I'm calm. My priorities aren't foggy."

"So, when you start feeling crazy, just go for a walk."

"I don't think it's quite that simple."

"I think I will be more patient for some things, less patient for others," Nic says thoughtfully. "What do you mean?"

"I feel like I can see a bigger picture. I don't mean that I've reached illumination or anything, I just feel like the petty things that people got stressed about were not important. I mean, I knew it before. I knew that the backstabbing idiocies of my teachers against the administration of my school were petty and wrong. But now my guttural distaste for it has really kicked in. Now I want to keep as far away as possible from that shit, like it were contagious."

"And what about stuff you'll be more patient towards?" he asks.

"I think I'll be more patient towards anyone making an effort to rise out of their suffering, to better themselves. I think I'll be more patient towards those people. No matter how messed up, no matter how imperfect. When I see that they're trying, I think I'll be able to realize how much it's costing them."

Natalie and Marta walk into the bar. We tell them what we're talking about. "I think I'm done with committees," Natalie says. I raise my glass to her.

"Amen, sister." I wonder if I can make such a promise, since I will return to my work in community services. Committees are more than just a means to an end, they are the marrow of life for us. Opting out of committees may not be an option.

Marta clears her throat. "Speaking of life changes, did you know I used to be a lawyer in Manhattan? Worked at a huge law firm, 60, 70 hours a week sometimes."

Natalie and I gawk at her. "But, Marta, you seem so calm ..." I say.

Marta nods and then tells us her twenty- to thirty-something life story. When Marta was at the height of her career, having made junior partner at a respectable law firm, travelling Europe on big cases and making more money than was humanly decent, she and her husband would escape New York City every Friday night and drive up to the Adirondacks for the weekend.

"No matter how late it was, no matter how tired, we'd just get in the car and drive four hours to our rental cottage," she said, "and I'm pretty sure it was the only thing keeping me sane."

One weekend, they wound up at an auction. A local resident had just passed away without any family, so he left his entire estate to a charitable organization, including his house, to be auctioned off. The auctioneer announced the house and no one put in any bid. The turn-of-the-century, six-bedroom somewhat rickety house was going for less than a studio apartment in Brooklyn.

The auctioneer closed up shop, house unsold, and made his way to the door. Marta and her husband looked at each other for a moment and then caught him on his way out.

Long story short, the property was theirs by the end of the week. She eventually quit her fancy job and took up teaching at a local community college. They now buy their eggs and milk from the farmer down the road and pay their grocer with checks, because he doesn't take debit.

"I'm not saying there's always a correlation between money and happiness," says Marta, "but here's the thing. The time in my life when I was making the most money I've ever made was also when I was the most unhappy. And I'm just saying, the time in my life when I was the happiest is right now, and I am making the least money I have ever made. Just saying."

"Oh my God," I say, "you're living the dream. You've made that huge life change that people make movies about. Why are you doing the Camino again? Haven't you already reached your answer?"

"I like travelling, Jenna!" laughs Marta, "and you can reach an answer in life, and still be asking more questions."

"That's amazing," sighs Natalie. "You've made all these changes, and I'm still trying to get over mine. I'm going to be at peace with all the changes in my life," she says pensively, and then looks over at me. "So am I to understand that you have reached your Camino answer?" she asks me.

I roll my eyes.

"Natalie, I'm not even sure I've articulated my Camino question. I mean how are you supposed to know what this walk is teaching you? I get up, I walk, I enjoy the scenery, I talk with you guys. The meseta is so mind-emptying, and I love that. But how am I supposed to apply that back home? When's the revelation supposed to happen?"

She nods. "Maybe all of it happens later. You notice some people totally changed their lives because of Santiago?"

I shudder. "Don't you find them a little weird? They kind of have googly eyes and speak in wispy voices."

"And don't forget about the job they give up, the multiple repeat Caminos they do, and all the hours they spend talking only of the wonders of the trail. Do you think they lost friends in the real world?" muses Nicolas.

"How do you decide what's healthy and what's not, though?" wonders Natalie. "I mean, far be it from me to tell someone they can't change their life. I met people who opened up inns and refuges along the way after reaching Santiago. They decide to devote their lives to hospitality and they're happy as clams. And look at Marta. She's happy."

I think about this and say, "I guess it's the difference between a true convert and a druggie. You've got those who experience something real and then change their lives in honor of what they lived. Then you've got those who experienced something real and spend the rest of their lives trying to repeat that high. It's like they can't adapt to living real life anymore. Everything is a search to imitate the feelings they had on the trail."

I don't admit as much, but I have all the potential to become a Camino druggie. Every time things become stressful at work, every time we can hear our neighbors too loudly at night, every parking ticket, every traffic jam in the hustle and bustle of urban living, I forget to be grateful for what I have. I forget that my job is fulfilling, that my apartment is comfortable, that my urban life is actually really fun. Moments of frenzy send me fantasizing about an alternative life, somewhere on a country farm raising chickens. Or running a B & B in southern France. Or sometimes it's a small apartment in downtown Paris as a writer. But I know that it's exactly that—a fantasy. Those dreams wouldn't work.

First of all, the chicken farm would be a lot of work and I wouldn't make enough money off the eggs to be able to install a more modern feeding coop. And the B & B in southern France would be problematic because I would end up having to host the French. And the apartment in downtown Paris is just a pipedream, because no writer save maybe John Grisham can afford an apartment in downtown Paris.

None of those situations, not one, can save me from moments of pain or loneliness or worry. And becoming a lifelong druggie of the Camino, seeking out those feelings of bliss, wouldn't save me from myself either. I'd end up fantasizing about returning to a job where I could actually contribute something to society rather than living a life of self-service. The true converts of the Camino are not interested in self-service.

Henri Nouwen, in *Reaching Out: The Three Movements of the Spiritual Life* writes that there is a spiritual movement that we all must seek, that being from illusion to prayer. Illusion is rooted in images of grandeur, fear, escapism or desires of immortality. Prayer centers us in reality, abandoning control and surrendering ourselves to God's care. There are two post-Camino states. The first one—that of the druggie, is set in illusion. The second is that of the true convert. It centers itself in the living prayer of practicing the lessons of peace learned on your pilgrimage in the face of turmoil, friendship in the face of hostility, and hospitality in the face of egotism.

I will try for the rest of my life, be it on busy days filled with committee meetings, or of picking up my next parking ticket, or on the next trail I walk in silence, to centre myself in the living prayer of a true Camino convert.

Chapter 31
Meltdown in Léon

The meseta gradually turns green, bit by bit, and soon we are only one day out from Léon. We are nearing the end. Léon means we are about twelve days from Santiago. I lose track of villages' names, of the meals we ate, of the inns or *refugios* where we stayed. I don't know what day of the week it is. My bag no longer feels heavy, my feet no longer have blisters, my body has finally taken the shape of the road. But in its comfort it has also become worn, weary and rough. Not one part of me feels fresh. I begin to understand the terms wiry and weather-beaten. This is what farmers must feel like after harvest.

We spend a day in Léon. We cheated, that is. Took the bus into town from Mansilla de los Mulas with Marta, Natalie and Mia, promising each other that one bus ride was not the end of the world, that there is no shame in skipping a step, that there should be no judgment towards those who take the shortcut. I'm fine with it. Nicolas needed a bit more convincing.

The day of tourism in Léon feels great. I eat octopus and tapas and ice cream. We walk the squares and visit the churches, and meet up with Camino friends. I am loving being in this city with its gorgeous restaurants and shops, everything so vibrant compared to the emptiness of the meseta. Life feels good. Until the next morning. We gather everything up and start walking to the edge of town. And then I stop. And burst into tears. "I can't go on! I can't do it!"

"Jen?!" Nicolas looks at me, wide-eyed and astonished. "What's the matter? Are you sick?"

"No, I'm not ill, I'm just fed up with walking," I sob, putting my head in my hands. I feel if I take one more step, I'll throw up.

"OK, Jen, you really don't look right. I think I need to take you to the doctor."

Nicolas' level of alarm, much to his annoyance, does the trick. I wipe my eyes and begin to laugh.

"The doctor? And what would you tell the doctor? 'Please fix my wife, she's crying?!?'"

"I don't know! You just don't seem right."

"Of course, I don't seem right! We've been walking for 53 days, I haven't slept in the same place more than two nights in a row, I am PMS-ing and now we need to go 30 kilometers through suburbia to get to our next destination." And I begin crying again.

"So let me get this straight ... this meltdown is because you're getting your period soon?"

I roll my eyes, "Is that the only thing you got out my whole speech?"

"Well it's really the only logical explanation."

I grab my bag. This is leading nowhere. "Come on. Let's go. My episode is over."

"Don't do that again. It scared me."

"Women cry, Nic."

"Don't I know it ..."

The Camino meltdown is a widely accepted condition on the road. The reasons why one would crack are many. Mine, it turns out, was the day of rest. Léon was the first time that I thought about the end of the journey. There was definitely more behind me than in front of me. My sleep was less restorative; it was more like a band-aid on an open wound. What I really needed were several days of deep, uninterrupted rest. I wouldn't get that for another two weeks, almost. My legs could go on. That wasn't my problem. But my head needed more convincing.

I rub my eyes a little and tell my poor bewildered husband that I am ready to go on. Several hours later we stop at a picnic table and pull out our lunch. Mia and Natalie wander up next to us.

"I had my meltdown today," I announce nonchalantly.

Natalie gasps. "Oh, no! You two were our inspiration! If you can't hold it together, then how will I?"

"Well, you don't really hold it together, mom," says Mia lightly.

"You're one to talk," retorts Natalie. "Has she ever told you what happens when we begin to see the day's destination? She systematically breaks into tears at the first glimpse of the town."

"Usually it's in the form of a church steeple, easy to spot from a distance because of its height," explains Mia. "If I see a steeple rising from a horizon, my legs turn to jelly and I get a lump in my throat. I think it's because I could taste the end of my day, but I know there's still a mile or two to go. My brain just thinks it won't handle it."

"She's like a Pavlovian dog!" laughs Natalie. "Show her a church steeple and she'll begin to wail."

"I'm feeling better now," I say hopefully. "But Léon was my church steeple, faintly visible beyond the horizon."

Nicolas still looks dazed. "What is it with women who just spontaneously burst into sobbing fits?"

"The Camino meltdown is no small thing, Nic," says Natalie. "It must be taken seriously."

I send her a grateful look and she winks at me. I can always count on her for an ally. Natalie had turned into a great friend. We'd helped her and Mia through the first week of walking when they were suffering from all the ailments that we had suffered in our first days, and now they in turn were making our last weeks go over smoothly; translating menus for us, telling us what foods to eat.

Natalie also had a marvelous ability—this tends to be a real American talent—to carry a conversation for hours on end with personal anecdotes, gossip, movie and book talk that provided some often badly needed distraction and entertainment on the road. I have noticed that on the days that we walked with Natalie and Mia my prayer times diminished but my social skills greatly improved.

"Come on," says Mia. "I know what will make you feel better. We'll sing our 'Camino musical' medley for you. We composed it yesterday on the road."

"I think my Camino meltdown might be about to begin," says Nic.

In my research on meltdowns, I read a great deal about athletes. In marathons, runners experience what they call " hitting the wall." There are different theories on what The Wall is all about, but most experts agree that it begins to occur at the last 6.2 miles of the 26-mile run. It also has something to do with glycogen depletion. Glycogen is basically glucose—energy, really—stored in the kidneys and liver. Once you've been running for 13.8 miles, your body uses it all up, and the runner is overcome by a sudden wave of exhaustion, pain and energy loss. But "hitting wall" occurs on some much deeper levels as well. There are accounts of runners breaking down in sobs, losing concentration, and feeling desperate. Sometimes they just get plain bored, which slows down the running.

On a larger, slightly metaphorical scale the pilgrim can experience the same thing. It may start with the physical—too many bad night's sleeps, food poisoning, an untreated muscle injury—but it rapidly descends into the psychological or spiritual. You begin hating walking. You feel homesick. You think you can't do it, you're too weak, you'll never get there. You're just plain fed-up.

Much worse than the physical injuries are the psychological states in which you begin to lose focus, lose your sense of purpose, lose yourself. Then you know you need to do something. In a marathon, it's a mind-over-matter situation. Coaches train runners to talk themselves out of their pain or despair. Some of them even pretend to be happy, knowing full well that this is an act. They do it anyway.

On the Camino, rest is probably the best thing, if possible, and when it's not, there's no match for a good sense of community. Meet the right people, or even the wrong people at the right time, and they will bring you through a multitude of sorrows. Or at least provide some healthy distraction.

The beauty of the road helps, but once you are fatigued, it no longer does the trick. And these days we were passing through many farms that had gotten a good deal of rain lately and the stench of rotting hay and wet manure hung above us in the air, like a thick ozone layer of reek. It was so awful it could make you gag. The asphalt stretches of the road were also particularly difficult. Not good for the tired soul.

But for me, going on was simply just a question of principle. I couldn't give up and certainly not give in to the emotion. We'd come too far, and I owed it to myself and to Nicolas. I had to just keep on showing up for the pilgrimage. Eventually the energy, the enthusiasm, and the desire caught up. But for the time being, it was just pure, raw, driven commitment.

The walk must go on.

Meltdown in Léon

Chapter 32
Sex and Other Complications

Yeah, not so much.

By the time we reach Astorga, on day 24 of Spain, and 55 of the Camino, and the Oh-boy-it's-been-a-while of our love life, I come to the conclusion that for being such a sacred experience, we don't get to know each other too much in the biblical sense. For one thing, you are never guaranteed a room for two. And even when you are, there's not that much in the mood-building department. Underwear soaking in the sink, legs being iced down in the bathtub, clothing and backpacks strewn on the floor, emitting various scents of the road.

It's like there's a dire need for intimacy with your mate, but once you find it, you don't get much past a good long hug. You're sitting on the bed, grateful for clean feet, fresh sheets, a pillow and a partner with whom you can hold hands. Which pretty much sums up my idea of a good life.

Some pilgrims have other ideas. "There are more bachelors on the road these days," says one busybody of a *hospitalero*. "I ask them if they mind being alone and they've told me that actually they are doing the Camino to meet women. Can you imagine?"

I can, actually. During the first week in Spain, we stopped at a magical inn in Villatuerta which is 500 years old and full of nooks and crannies and spiraling staircases and hammocks and art deco tiles. The owner, Manuel, is soft and ageless and touches people on their elbows and feet. People say they melt at his touch, feel healed by it, that it evokes memories and emotions. They pay him for massages and for medical sessions where he treats their blisters and disinfects their cuts and tells them to respect their bodies, they must listen to their bodies, for their body is a temple. They emerge from his massage room looking starry-eyed and dreamy.

Sean, our experienced Camino friend, says he would pay to be a fly on the wall during one of his sessions, just to see what goes on that makes his clients feel so utterly moved and cared for. "He probably just hypnotizes them and then lights up a cigarette for the remainder of the hour," he jokes dryly.

Manuel's wife is a much younger version of him, soft and relaxed and helpful, and when people tell her that his touch is magical, she smiles shyly and says, "That's why I stayed." She apparently was a little *peregrina* herself until stopping at the inn. One night with Manuel, and her Camino ended right then and there.

We meet Emmy and her brother Peter, the two inseparable Flemish pilgrims, the darlings of the trail to all older pilgrims. Family love, it really is sweet. Emmy is a killer walker, out-walking everyone including Peter, who is quite athletic. A few weeks later, though, on our day in Astorga, we see Emmy in front of Gaudí's Episcopal Palace in the arms of a burly stout pilgrim by the name of Han.

"Oh, a new man!" I say to her and she winks at me. "Where's your brother?"

She shrugs, "I have no idea. He said he got sick of waiting for me and Han and that he'd see me in Santiago."

"He dumped you?!"

She looks at me a bit sheepishly. Her fling had broken up the dynamic sibling duo. Last I heard she had fallen behind me and Nicolas as well.

The canoodling certainly dampened her pace. Of course, I call it a fling, but you never know. I have a friend back home who met the love of her life on the way to Santiago di Compostella, and to boot, they are still together. Although married, he left his native Spain to come and start a new life with his fellow *peregrina*.

Nicolas and I have been married for six years. We're not on the trail for any sort of honeymoon (although we met a couple of crazies who were doing just that) nor to find some sort of sexual escapade, nor to rekindle any died out romance.

However.

The lack of domestic duty was nice on both of us. As was the absence of everyday stress caused by jobs, calls from our mothers, doctor's appointments or a landlord's botched repair of the balcony. We fell into an easy entre-deux of voyage, carefreeness and nonstop conversation because of all the time we were spending together. This doesn't mean there were no fights. It turns out even without the stress of everyday life, couples can find plenty to fight about.

For us, it's money and walking rhythms. He gets furious with me for not planning our spending better; I get furious with him for being impatient and stressed. He walks faster, wants to leave earlier; I would like to enjoy the morning for a while longer over a cup of coffee. I say he's too impatient; he says I complain too much. We've begun playing Camino Bingo, in which we can dole out a new letter (B-I-N-G-O) every time our partner is whining. I've gotten my fair share of letters. I don't dare say a word about my uncomfortable bag strap anymore, for fear of getting a B. And on and on it goes.

He makes another worried comment about the budget, and we finally have it out—calmly. Walking the Camino at least taught us how to confront in a Zen-like manner. "I will not entertain your stress about money anymore," I say to him.

"Jen, I just want you to be more careful. I don't ever want for us to go without ..."

"And when has that ever happened? You budget, re-budget, over budget. We left with enough money for two Caminos. We're staying in an abbey for six euros a night. And yet I can still feel you getting heart palpitations every time we go to a restaurant."

"If we do everything you want, we'll run out. Doesn't this worry you?"

"No."

It's not that I never worry about money. I overspent for awhile on my credit card in my early twenties and worried a whole lot about money then, but what with Nicolas feeling so stressed all the time around finances, I think I became more relaxed by default.

My family never had much growing up, and somehow we always managed. Clothes (albeit not many), a car (never anything fancy), summer vacations (a whole lot of camping, but a few exotic trips here and there) and food on the table (and many, many leftovers). What can I say? My parents are generous. They pick up the tab when we eat out together, they give to charity, they always arrive with elaborate gifts at baby showers.

I just never grew up with the sense that we were lacking. I only learned later on that for the first ten years of my life, we lived very nearly below the poverty line. We didn't own a house until the third baby was born. And I seem to remember a certain minuscule rusted junk bucket of a car being our main mode of transport up until I finished the third grade. Even then I had no knowledge of us being somewhat strapped for cash. So worrying about loads of things in life comes naturally to me, but worrying about money doesn't.

"We're not going to run out of money," I tell Nicolas curtly. "You know why? Because you won't let us. You're magnificent with money. You have financially planned us into the future so well that you've all but set up a trust fund for a child that we aren't even sure we are going to have. So with someone like that in my life, why would I worry? And you shouldn't worry either. Because you're in your life. And you're doing a really good job of taking care of things."

Nic sighs and for a minute. I can see him trying to argue back. And then in a rare moment of surrender, he says, "I suppose you want to go for a tapas run?"

"And ice cream, please."

Here is the most wonderful, sexiest thing about Nicolas. If you speak to him logically, with words and arguments that make sense, he will not only give in but actually change his mind.

Not like me. I'll self-defend to the point of madness. Thank goodness, I had the good sense to marry someone who has a great deal more good sense than I do.

Sex and Other Complications

Chapter 33
Relics

Two days later, we enter Ponferrada, our last big urban area before we reach Santiago. "There's a great castle here, belonged to the Templars. And I think they have a museum of relics in the next town," Nic says to me.

"Let me guess ... splinters from the cross and tears of the Virgin."

"Something like that."

There are so many churches in Europe that boast of these two relics that we could probably build a forest out of all the splinters from the cross and fill a dried-up well from the tears of the Virgin Mary. The mother of God was seemingly quite emotional and a had a number of bad days.

"At least it's not a piece of Jesus' foreskin," says Nic.

"Don't remind me," I reply.

In Conques, we went to the museum next to the monastery, the one that held the "treasure of Conques," that is, Saint Faith's remains, and many other ancient relics from France's earliest days of Christianity. One was "Le prépuce de l'enfant Jésus"—Baby Jesus' foreskin. "Do you really mean to tell me that in that ornate box we can find a piece of Jesus' penis?" I ask Nic.

"Apparently."

"Pure and utter crap."

"Hey, I'm just reading the card."

"You mean to tell me that when Jesus was eight days old and his parents took him to the temple to get circumcised, that mother Mary said to the rabbi, 'Oh wait, would you mind if I held onto that, because you know, when he becomes famous and all in 33 years, some church up in northern France may want a piece of this?'

"And how did she preserve it? Don't you think she'd be cleaning out the house one day when Jesus was, say, 12 years old and be like, 'What the heck is this? Eww ... toss that.'

"Jenna, you do realize the Church doesn't much recognize these objects any more, right? It's more like a silent tolerance of them as historical and cultural artifacts, but you'd be hard-pressed to find a bishop who would publicly affirm that this little golden box actually holds a piece of Jesus' penis, let alone that it would have a any spiritual or religious powers."

"Well, I'm glad to hear that, but doesn't this whole charade around relics bother you a bit as a Catholic?"

"Not really. Every government in history needed its assets. I'm not saying the Catholic Church was any better than the lords of the land, but they certainly weren't worse. I mean, they were building a culture. The Church and the state built entire cities around relics. If you said you had the elbow of a saint, there would be armies and royalty and nobility who would traipse out to your neck of the woods. Cha-ching! They'd have money and influence to finish monasteries, cathedrals. They'd get armed protection ..."

"This is what I'm saying. Your so-called saint's elbow was a tool to manipulate economy and power."

"OK, but you're only looking at it from one side. What about all the parishioners who couldn't read, who had no access to the Bible? They needed objects. Something tangible. Some material representation of their beliefs.

"Think about how mundane their lives were. These were peasants, farmers. They'd probably never even left their town in their whole lives. Then in comes this priest who says, 'I have a finger of Saint Peter.' It's like for the first time the presence of something sacred and mystical is in their midst. Not only that, but this piece of global Christendom is being brought into their tiny existence. The Christians of the day couldn't go to Jerusalem. So, through the relics, Jerusalem came to them."

"It doesn't justify the lie."

"You can't prove that even the higher authorities of the time knew it was a lie. That they knew if the fingers—or even Jesus' penis—were fakes. You're thinking like a modern, rational being where everything can be disproved, explained away. They didn't think like that. A knight waltzes in and gives a piece of wood to the parish priest and tells him it's a gift from the king and it's a piece of the cross. The priest is pretty excited. They didn't ask questions. They WANTED to believe. And it created village pride. Patriotism. 'Looky here, you barbarian Germanics, we've got a piece of the cross! Yeah!'"

"So what do Christians do about all of these objects of doubtful historical legitimacy?"

"Well, like I said, you'd be hard-pressed to find a priest today ready to die defending the authenticity of most of these objects ..."

"So having Jesus' penis as part of the church treasury isn't that important?"

"I wouldn't think so. But look at it this way. Why are we on this pilgrimage?"

"To walk the Camino."

"Wrong! Historically speaking, we're actually off to see the remains of Santiago, the very Saint James himself, and to pay homage to his remains in the Cathedral of Compostella. Is it really his body? We don't know. Do his remains have some special, gravitational spiritual force? I wouldn't think so. But the point is, this road wouldn't be here without him."

Actually, to add a twist to this strange piece of Church history, the relics of Santiago may be more real than cynics care to admit. Legend has it that the Apostle James, son of Zebedee, was a missionary to Iberia (modern-day Spain and Portugal) after Christ's ascension. How someone back in AD 70 made their way up to northern Spain from Jerusalem is a little beyond me, but there you have it.

There are also these very glamorous and epic stories about how James is the original conqueror of the Moores. He rode his horse into battle and slaughtered the army. This was supposed to have been a glorious legend at the time, but now it just looks like a dark tale of ethnic cleansing.

History tells us that James went back to Judea where he was martyred by Herod. His disciples, however, decided to take his remains and bury him in the land that had been so shaped by his missionary work, making Galicia his final resting place. (Legend also has it that in bringing his body back to Spain, the boat which carried it was lost at sea, and thousands of seashells rose to the surface of the water, floating him to the shores of Spain. Thus the seashell became the everlasting symbol of a pilgrim on the Way of Saint James).

Fact and fiction, history and fable became muddled and melded into one tale, and it is difficult to discern what is real and what is not. However, in 1988, the Spanish diocese decided to undertake an excavation of the Cathedral of Santiago, in anticipation of the Pope's visit to Spain. They discovered a tiny third-century chapel and a crypt in which three stone coffins were uncovered. Lo and behold, Tada!, and what would you know, the inscriptions on the coffins were of a Jerusalem dialect that dated back to AD 80.

Historians may disagree on many a matter, but on this one they all admit that it necessarily had to be someone from Jerusalem in the era of the Apostle James and Jesus buried there. It is impossible that it could have been a Spaniard of the time. So there you have it: Every now and then some quirky fact rises from the relics' safe box and slaps you in the face. In Santiago's case, it was an eerily accurate inscription on his coffin that fits the story of his death and burial.

But Nicolas is getting at a whole other level of meaning. "Yup," he continues, "all of Western Europe, and especially France and Spain, can thank their Medieval ancestors for believing in relics because without them we wouldn't have this awesome road."

"So you're saying the relics are OK?"

"I'm saying the culture that grew out of them—maybe without the Crusades, those weren't too cool—was OK. We wouldn't have some of our most beautiful art, our best pilgrimages, without the relics. I'm saying God is capable of taking something as crappy as a make-believe Baby Jesus penis that was used for money, greed and power, and redeem it by turning it into a vessel of truth and a journey of belief."

Relics

Chapter 34
O'Cebreiro

I have walked into a cloud. Right now, Madrid's temperature varies around 93 degrees Fahrenheit, with siesta hitting 105. I, on the other hand, am shivering from the cold and have lips turned blue from freezing. Ladies and gentlemen, you are in Galicia.

O'Cebreiro is the door into Galicia. We arrive there on the night of my birthday and our anniversary, after a day of ascension deep into the Galician mountains. The more we climbed, the foggier the air got. Natalie and Mia walked with us, making their usual coffee and pastry stops every two miles or so.

"This trip has so many hidden expenses," says Natalie after our third cafe stop of the day. I sip my cafe con leche and concur.

Up, up and away. All day we climb, all day it gets more and more gray. I literally cannot see thirty feet in front of me. "Have we died? Is this the afterlife?" I ask out loud.

I can tell there are mountains all around me, and I know from the guidebook that there are drops of 300 yards down. But ask me if there are people behind me, and I wouldn't have the faintest clue. All we can see is the path below our feet. The road is soft and mossy, the air damp, and the greenery thick and lush. We are a far cry from the meseta.

By afternoon, the rain begins. It trickles silently onto the moss-covered stone walls of farmhouses and roads. We need to hurry up and get to O'Cebreiro before we become too wet. We hear a faint sound of bagpipes in the distance, and we turn a corner and there are some stone steps. We climb the steps and find ourselves in AD 900.

There really aren't enough ways to describe the impression one gets of O'Cebreiro. You enter another era, another land. Gone are the multicolored Spanish houses, gone are the balconies of potted fire-red geraniums, tiled facades, strings of lights and vibrant cafe bars we'd grown so accustomed to in Spain. We are now in Middle Earth. Or in Medieval Ireland.

My first impressions aren't so far off. First of all, Galicia is considered one of the Celtic nations of Western Europe, due to its distinctly Celtic culture, so different from the rest of Spain. Historians believe that this region was inhabited by the Galician peoples, who spoke a Celtic dialect, since the Bronze Age, until the Romans annexed the territory. The dialects died out, but the national identity remained.

Natalie unpacks this for me. "About five years ago, I had a nanny who was Galician. I used to ask her about Spanish culture and she was unable to tell me much about bullfighting, flamenco, or siesta hour. Her world was Celtic, from the folklore to the music to the highland games. It was so bizarre, speaking to a seemingly Latin teenager who was more immersed in bagpipes and four-leaf clovers than in the cultures of Barcelona or Madrid."

Bagpipes are what you get here, and wispy green valleys with snow-capped mountains in the winter, misty air, and bulky stone pathways. O'Cebreiro is something of an open-air museum, its architecture and layout so well-preserved and remembered through the centuries. It's a village which up until about a hundred years ago still had a somewhat Medieval way of life. O'Cebreiero is built around the church of Saint Mary whose foundations date the pre-Romanesque era. The chalice and baptismal pool are still original, but the remainder of it has been rebuilt. The rest of the village is made up of brown and gray stone hotels, restaurants and inns, and their famous pallozas.

A palloza is Roman-style roundhouse, the main part made of stone, and the roofs cone-shaped and thatched. Most of the pallozas have been rebuilt (thatched roofs don't last that long), but there are a few remaining pallozas that were built on some very old foundations.

Is O'Cebreiro authentic in its aesthetic and history? In so far as original Medieval hamlets that are a magnet for tourists can be, yes. But truly, historically accurate or not, O'Cebreiro is magical, with its stone walkways, thatched roofs, misty surroundings, and strong fireplaces. I wanted to have a pint and wait for Gandalf to join us.

Pint it was and Caldo Gallego to follow. That is, after we went to our hotel room, and peeled off our clothes, took a hot shower, put on our only change of dry clothes (which, after being in our bags all day, were kind of cold and humid) and ran through the rain, feeling our way to the bar which was hard to see from any sort of distance because of the fog. After all that, we had Caldo Gallego.

Caldo Gallego is a Galician soup that has become a staple for pilgrims in these parts, because it's hearty, full of protein, and hot. And in this region, in between the dampness, the cold and the ascensions, you need it.

When making Caldo Gallego, it is important to remember that you are working with ingredients that come straight from a Galician farm. More precisely, you are working with leftovers of ingredients from a Galician farm, so nothing is an exact science. This is a hearty rustic stew, not a Parisian soufflé, so you can play around with the portions and elements. Don't like turnips? Don't put them in! Want more bacon flavor? Of course you do! Who doesn't want more bacon? Throw more in! Want to play around with the variations of chorizo? Do it!

Here are the guidelines:

2 garlic cloves, crushed
1 large onion, chopped

1 piece of pork back fat (About a 3-inch piece should do. Ask your butcher for this.)

2 cups of dried white kidney beans, soaked overnight and boiled for one hour, OR 3 cans of white kidney beans. (Hint: If you want a fresher, more authentic taste, go for soaking the beans. If you don't mind your broth being a bit thicker and frothier, go for the canned beans.)

3 large russet potatoes, peeled and cubed

2 cups of collard greens or spinach, cut into bite-sized pieces. (You can also use turnip greens. Remember, this is a "throw whatever's left over into the pot" recipe, so if it's green, it should do!)

1 large turnip, peeled and cubed

1 large ham hock

2 chorizo sausages

1/2 lb. slab of bacon, unsliced

Directions:

1. In a large pot, sauté the garlic cloves and the onion in the back fat over medium high heat until the garlic and onions are translucent. Add the cooked beans and 6-8 cups of water. Add the potatoes, turnips, all meat (uncut) and collard greens and bring to a boil. (If you are using spinach, add it later as it does not take as long to cook.)

2. Once boiling, lower the heat and let simmer for 35-40 minutes. Test the vegetables and the ham hock to see if they are cooked.

3. If everything is cooked, keep the soup simmering and remove the ham hock, bacon, back fat and chorizo.

4. Slice the chorizo into small pieces and return to the pot. Remove the fat from the bacon, slice the pink meat into cubes and add to the pot. Stir.

5. Remove the outer layer of the ham hock and string the meat off the bone with a fork, returning the strings of meat to the pot. (The bone can be kept for another soup!) Remove any small pieces of meat from the back fat and add them to the soup. The broth should be white and slightly creamy. If it's too thick, add water, adjusting the taste with salt.

6. Serve in large bowls, with toasted bread.

Nicolas and I returned to our room through the fog and sheets of rain. We snuggled down under blankets, our teeth chattering, trying to warm up. It was my birthday, and our wedding anniversary.

"Sorry it's not sunny, Jen," Nic said.

"Are you kidding?" I replied. "We're in medieval fairyland, I just ate the most fantastic stew of my life, we have a bottle of wine and a room without any snorers. I couldn't be happier. Happy anniversary, hon."

Nicolas squeezed my hand and we held each other, shivering, cold, and hilariously happy.

We left O'Cebreiro the next morning, and spent the next couple of days in the same sort of scenery, making our way down through mountainous paths and tiny Galician hamlets, through eucalyptus forests, walking on roads sheltered by moss-covered stone walls overlooking lush foggy valleys where cows and sheep graze. The smells varied from fresh wet grass to moldy hay.

I thought about all that I had seen since starting out. French countryside, UNESCO landmarks, the Pyrenees, the Spanish flatlands, and now, land that looked like Merlin's summer home.

All joined together by one road.

O'Cebreiro

Chapter 35
My Twenties

I woke up on the morning of my thirtieth birthday (and my sixth wedding anniversary) and realized I had bookended my twenties with elaborate trips to Europe.

On the day of my twentieth birthday, I was in Vienna with my sister and grandfather. It was a gorgeous day. I was dressed in pink, a light pink baby tee with a summer floral skirt and some beige sandals with pink and violet flowers embroidered onto them. My paternal grandfather, who adores me and whom I adore, took us out to a wonderful restaurant and to a concert—I think it was all Mozart—with the orchestra all dressed in period costumes. I had just ended a year as a student in Paris, and after Austria and a trip to Romania, I would be headed home.

Home. That was the worst part of the birthday. The looming unexpected elements of having to find a life for myself back at home. The plan, ever since high school, had been for me to spend a year studying abroad. I had never thought past that plan. The year abroad took up all my financial planning, all my interest, all my imagination. Now that it was over, I would have to return to normalcy, and I had no idea where I was headed.

I had gotten into the faculty of music at Université de Montréal, turning down studies in other faculties, mainly because I was too scared not to do music. I was afraid that if I didn't pursue my instrument, then I would never be at the level of excellence I wanted to be at. I had worked so hard for so long at the violin that I couldn't afford not to keep on going, without considering for a minute all that I would give up if I did.

I would learn that lesson the hard way. To be sure, I would reach a certain level of artistic excellence over the course of the next four years, although never the level I really wanted, nor the level that a career in music would necessitate, and it would come at a steep cost to my own self-image, my stress levels and my feelings of self-worth.

If I had really wanted to care for myself, nurture myself in my studies, I should have marched myself out of that music faculty after the first day of ensemble auditions, when I watched girls run out of studios crying into handkerchiefs. I should have gone straight to Admissions and switched my Bachelor's to classics, or literature or theology. Or music history. Anything but violin performance. Then I could have spent four years in the library with my nose in books, instead of in the practice rooms, trembling fingers on the violin, killing myself to master double stops and four-octave scales and orchestral excerpts during my Christmas break for the auditions in January. (I almost always came in last).

I was also heading back into a relationship that I wasn't sure I wanted, but that I would stay in for far too long, because it seemed right. Because it looked good. Because, once more, I was afraid of not sticking it out. Afraid I would be making a mistake if I left. I wasn't ready for this person (and he certainly wasn't ready for me) and I knew deep down I didn't really want this, but I would take it none the less.

When I headed back, I would take on a schedule that was not humanly possible because I was afraid of missing out on some great project, some great connection, some great opportunity. Everything I did during the first couple of years in my twenties was done out of fear of being left behind in a world of mediocrity, when what I really wanted was achievement and greatness.

I made my choices in my twenties, but they were made somewhat blindly, under the spell of society telling young women they need to do more, be more, achieve more. I would pay the price for those choices.

Of course I didn't know any of this on the day I turned 20, but I did have, in the evening, a great feeling of sadness and a certain premonition of leaving something behind on that day. And so I cried. Crying because I didn't want to leave, crying because I didn't want to go back, crying because I was clinging to my childhood while desperately seeking my independence. And so I started out my twenties in tears.

Were my twenties all that bad? Of course not. I studied, travelled, got my own apartment with Victorian moldings, a chores chart for the roommates and solid red walls to match the second-hand furniture. I got out of one bad relationship that sent me gasping for air, and into a really good one.

I decided to marry the good one after he asked me why I could be so brave with him when I was so cowardly with everyone else on earth. "I don't get. You never take any crap from me, you always take me on and disagree and put up an argument and claim your intellectual turf. But then I see you with others ... you turn into a doormat. What's up with that?" I told him I didn't know, but that if he was the only one I could do that with, I'd better hold on to him, and so we got married.

But in all, my twenties were chock-full of busyness and of pressure and of stories of me not standing up for myself to others, mainly other women. I met a lot of women who don't help other women, especially younger ones in this world. I met women, insecure and obsessed, who walked all over the younger ones, suspicious of them, mistrusting them and then making them prove themselves. It wasn't until a bit later that I was able to seek out the wonderful women in my life, the wise, beautiful, intelligent creators and movers and shakers whom I look up to and can follow down those lovingly sculpted paths that were so difficult to pave.

But that was later. In my early twenties, I was tortured. Tortured over every decision that came my way, and there were a load of them; tortured over every bully who was daring me to prove myself; tortured over my feelings of unworthiness and incompetence; tortured over my religion and my upbringing and my family.

Then I turned 29. Something changed. I finished my Master's. I didn't go to meetings thinking that I needed to shut up and disappear for fear of other people finding out how stupid I was. I managed my schedule better, which was a direct result of my ability to say no. I realized my religion and upbringing and family weren't bad, just quirky. Quirky can be good. Quirky leads to loving acceptance. I began to walk. I walked to church, I walked to my Quaker's meetings, I walked the Mont-Royal, I walked. And I began to feel the era of my twenties behind me.

I was standing in a tapas bar in Logrono when I explained to Ann, who was also 29, my feelings of serenity at turning 30, which would happen in about three weeks. She smiled shyly, "I know exactly what you mean. My birthday is only in March, but I've been telling people that I'm already 30. I can't wait."

On the day I turned 30, we were in O'Cebreiro. When we left on this trip I thought by the beginning of July, having walked something like 1,000 miles by then that I would have lost, say, 10 pounds and would have started out the era of my thirties with a shape I hadn't had in years—a little less flab, everything a bit more toned and firm. That's another thing with women in their twenties, or many other ages, come to think of it. We torture ourselves with how we look.

I thought that I would be losing weight on the trail. This was before I began eating all the French cheeses, the four-course meals, the salty carbs in Spain that I would consistently crave midday. I'll be lucky if I can maintain my weight let alone lose any. So really, on the day I turned 30, I might have lost weight, might have gained it. Who knows? And while my muscles were more toned and a bit firmer, my veins were also popping out from all the hard work.

All this to say, I have no idea how much I weighed on the day I turned 30 and I have no idea if I looked fabulous and athletic, or simply half-crazed and worn out, albeit with some really awesome muscles. No one around me could objectively tell either, because they also had been walking hundreds of miles and looked just as bad, or good, or whatever. And I didn't care. I can't remember the last time I woke up in the morning not knowing how much I weighed and not caring how I looked.

And then Nicolas said something that made me laugh. I can't remember what it was, but I do remember thinking that I was happy to wake up next to someone who made me laugh. And then I remember thinking, "I started my twenties by crying, but I started my thirties by laughing."

My Twenties

Chapter 36
Roman

Nicolas and I met Roman (pronounced *Roe-Mann* in Spanish) in the town of Molinaseca. I can safely say that Roman will be the last new friend I make. We are little more than one week out from Santiago, and we met him in one of the last quiet stops along the road. I decide I have room for just one more acquaintance, and Roman gets the prize.

Roman has silver hair and a mustache to match. He also wears lots of gold rings. I have yet to see him without a cigarette in his hands, and the image of this wine-loving, chain-smoking womanizer hiking the mountains of Galicia in a dirty white tank top and a sports backpack is almost too good for words, but I shouldn't laugh. This is his third Camino. The bling man could teach me a lesson or two, the first of which is to quit taking the Camino so seriously.

"This weather not so good." He says to me on the first day I meet him. "Tomorrow, I gonna take the bus."

I gonna take the bus. In the short time I knew Roman, I must have heard that phrase 62 times. "Ah, chica, today there are too many people on the road. Is a parade, not a Camino. Tomorrow, I gonna take the bus."

But he never did. Of course, he had a point about all the people. The road had already become a bit busier since Leon, and in every town we stopped in now, we gained more and more people walking the road. We had suffered an especially trying night in Triacastalla, which was day 60, after 40 Boy Scouts marched into our albergue. Aged around 13 to 15, in uniform, and always prepared, these little helpers of humankind took over the common area, monopolized the courtyard and were seemingly incapable of treading lightly on their dorm room floor, which was one floor directly above our heads. After 20 minutes of creaking, stomping, shuffling, squeaking, Nicolas gave an authoritative cough and said, "Well, I think it's time to bring out the old high school teacher act."

"No, Nicolas, don't!"

"Why not?"

"For one, they've got their Scout leaders with them to calm them down, and furthermore, you don't speak enough Spanish!"

"Oh, Jenna, please let him go," said Marta, in the bed next to ours. The poor girl was suffering from a sunburn and a headache, and I think the forty Scouts were bit much, even for her quiet, patient nature.

Nic headed up, and within an instant the voices muffled and the shuffling quieted down to a mere sigh.

He came back into the room looking rather pleased with himself. "Never underestimate the power of body language," he says. "One stern look from me and we'll get peace." Right then, one of the Scouts farted loudly and the other 39 reacted in an appropriate uproar. We were done in for the night.

I recounted our night to Ramon over cafe con leche the next morning, trying to take in enough caffeine so as to wake myself up.

He laughed good and hard and then said, " Ah, chica. Yesterday was a hard day. I am walking and a girl falls in front of me. Break the leg. I carry her bag until next village. Then we call the ambulance. Her bag was heavier than mine. Because, you know, is woman's bag and you need all the hair shit. Ah, chica ..." That sort of chip on his shoulder disappeared as soon as he was required to help someone.

Roman was my quintessential Spaniard. I half-expected him to whip out a bolero and begin to flamenco in front of me. But of course, if he did that, he'd have to drop the cigarette. And moving quickly was something that Roman did not take kindly to. I did not, in two solid weeks, pass a bar without seeing Roman sitting at the table sipping his cafe con leche and having a puff. Most of the time, it was too sweet an image to not join in.

"You always eating," he says to me as I stuff my face with a croissant. I look up bashfully. "You think you gonna lose weight with all the walking, but is not the case. You walk, you stop and eat. You walk, you stop and eat." He throws his head back and howls in laughter.

"A North American man would never say that to a woman," I tell him and I feel Nicolas, wide-eyed, nod his head behind me.

"Relax, baby. Here, it's a compliment. A woman who eats is beautiful. Except if she eats too much, then she costs her husband money."

A group of walkers pass us by smiling and waving. "Hi, Roman!" He lifts his hand. "Everybody so nice on the Camino." He comments, pronouncing his v's like b's. *Eberybody*. "You go home, you become a bitch. But on the Camino, you bery nice."

One of the last times we saw Roman was in a cafe in Sarria. Sarria is an especially challenging spot for those of us who have been at it a month or more. To obtain the Compostella (the pilgrim's certificate) from the pilgrim's office of Santiago, you have to prove you walked at least 65 miles. Sarria is the closest point to the 65-mile mark, and therefore all those pilgrims who want to get their Compostellas without doing the entire trek start out in Sarria. There are entire streets in Sarria dedicated to the lodging, feeding and guiding of these new pilgrims. The old guard, we Camino snobs, stare them down in disdain.

Roman, whom we met up with at a small restaurant in the heart of town, was the worst: "What is all this new people here? This is terrible! Tomorrow, I gonna take the bus."

We order from the waiter. Being now well into Galicia, one of the culinary specialties is *pulpo,* octopus. The menu (if you can call it that;

it's really just a small list scribbled on a chalk board) is octopus pulled fresh out of the tank, boiled, cut up, and seasoned right before our eyes, along with chunks of lamb, grilled and seasoned, and served on a slab of thick mahogany-colored wood, home-baked bread, slapped down on the table with a large butcher's knife sticking out of the middle of the unsliced loaf, cheese (as with the bread, one huge wheel, slapped down with a knife) and wine at two euros a bottle, which the waiter slides down the bar with two cups.

That's it. It was bar none, the BEST food I had in all of Galicia, and the atmosphere was amongst the brightest. Roman uses a toothpick to stab pieces of meat and octopus, savoring each piece. He calls over the waiter and asks him for mustard.

"Mostaza?" The waiter shrugs, showing he clearly has no idea.

"He's never heard of mustard?" I ask Roman.

Roman shakes his head, "Is not so common here." He rolls his eyes as the waiter brings him ketchup. "No! No catzup! Mostaza, mostaza! Catzup, no! Mayonesa, no! Mostaza!"

The waiter returns with the manager, who holds a passionate discourse with Roman. Finally, the manager's eyes light up. "Ah, si!" and he scuttles away, returning in an instant with a bottle of mayonnaise. I burst out laughing.

"Arh, chica. What country is that they don't eben know what is mustard? So closed minded. Tomorrow, I gonna take the bus."

Chapter 37
The Body

The first thing I wrote in my journal at the end of the first day was that my body was a huge disappointment to me. My mind of course is eons ahead of what my physicality can do. I was frustrated at the discomfort I was feeling, the pain and aches that were holding me back.

There are so many historical tales of the early Camino pilgrims and their physical suffering. They had much less comfort than we do. No soft, warm beds for the lower classes, no magical shoes, ergonomic equipment, rainproof windbreakers. Water sources were not as common. Wolves and wild rabid dogs were much more of a threat. Your chances of dying on the Camino di Santiago were just a whole lot higher.

Typically, depending on the threads of theology that each pilgrim adhered to, if they suffered more, they sacrificed more, and if they sacrificed more, they would be drawn closer to God. The body, or rather the denial of bodily comforts, was the sign of a true pilgrim, one who had really earned his reward at the end.

We have in contemporary Christianity gone to great lengths to reject this particular theology, that scorns the age of the penitent monk. Of course I do not condone the intentional self-destruction of the body for any reason, least of all on religious grounds, but I do think we may have lost something in ignoring what a body can do for somebody's spiritual development.

I don't understand, nor would I ever want to, the voluntarily imposition of physical suffering as a means to prove one's spiritual worth. I do understand, however, how physical pain and lack of material comforts can deepen your spirituality. You are closer to the earth. When you are in pain, you forget about trivial distractions. You are dependent upon the kindness of others and the grace of God to sustain you and provide for your needs.

It is very simple: You are no longer self-sufficient. Your money isn't providing an easy way out, you have no possessions that could possibly use to your well-being. There were certain villages along the way that simply didn't have fancy hotels or elaborate pharmacies. You simply had to make do. Your body, and as a consequence, the outcome of your Camino, are both at the mercy of factors that you have little control over.

Most books about the Camino warn of the body's breakdown, and the hits it might have to take from dangers like tendinitis, dehydration, muscle strain, food poisoning. They describe these bad outcomes as things to be avoided, which of course is true. It was like a balancing act between unavoidable risk and staying healthy. But nothing I read described the gift of the body, all the wonderful things the body gave forth to our Camino, all of its contributions to our experience.

I could (and did) spend time cursing my body, its shortcomings and failings, but the body is such an important part of the road. We can't attain our initial objectives—peace of mind, spiritual well-being, community—without it. If you don't walk, you don't learn. If your body isn't cooperating, you can't get to the walking. The point of the walk was not to deny or improve the body, but my body became an intrinsic part of both my denial and improvement. It was not the point of the exercise to induce suffering for its own sake. But in suffering, I learned that God doesn't command pain and hurt to overcome us. But it was in my hurt and pain that I drew closer to God.

My body is the vessel of the lessons of the pilgrimage, but my body is also the lesson in and of itself. It teaches me to rest when I feel tired, even when I want to go on. It instructs me to lay aside my ego, for if I do not, it will not be able to keep up. What I mean by that is, I met people along the way who had let their egos take over. They had forgotten to hold their feet and legs in the highest respect, treating them like some abused workhorse: just whip him a bit more, and he'll go that extra mile.

Typically these ego walkers were men aged 18 to 25. Pilgrims would watch them fall by the side of the road in exhaustion or with muscular damage and would whisper to each other in hushed tones, "The Camino still has some lessons to teach him." I would look at those guys in fear, because I know that I have it in myself to be every bit as self-destructive and egotistical. So I promise myself I will respect my muscles and tendons, my sunburn-prone skin, my neck and shoulders that can get sore. I promise to stop when I need to, to drink enough water, to stock up on sun-block.

My body teaches me to stop loathing its imperfections, the wrinkles, the bulges, blemishes and pimples. I cannot waste any time loathing the imperfections because whatever time I do have I must spend on tenderly caring for it, making sure it is well hydrated, soothed, cushioned and clean. It teaches me to love.

"Hey," say my legs before supper, "What are you doing? You may be happy to be here, but we're not OK. You need to take off those socks and soak your feet in warm water. If you don't, we won't be able to keep our end of the deal tomorrow." So I stop for a minute and soak my feet.

"Excuse me," my stomach pipes up, "I know you think that if you only eat fruit today, you could lose a few more ounces of fat. But you need that fat. If you don't feed me lots of calories, I will not take care of your muscles. I will put you in a bad mood. I will give you a headache and make you feel tired. So don't you dare look in the mirror one more time. Go to the cafe and order some eggs."

So I do. I gorge myself on tortillas con patatas and cafe con leche and breads, hungrily scarfing down the carbs, absorbing the vitamins, minerals, sugars and oils, as a diver would gasp for air as he rose to the surface of a lake. My body was happy. "Thanks, hon. You can keep on going now."

Two or three days after I finished my pilgrimage, I am sitting on a rock in the shallow part of the Atlantic Ocean, feeling the cold waves splash against my feet. I am feeling fragile, woozy, as though if I took too great a step, my innards might fall out. I am seized for a moment with feelings of both amazement and horror, grief and wonder, at what I had done to my body. I realized just how much I did to myself, just how far I had pushed myself, how many uncomfortable situations I had just endured. How badly things could have gone, even though they didn't.

I clutch my abdomen and hug my thighs. "I'm sorry," I tell them. "I'm so sorry at what I just put you through." Then a moment later, I feel a sense of relief and gratitude wash over me. I think about a priest back home who made pastoral visits to paraplegics and amputees. He spoke to us about those who would do a Camino but only in their souls and minds, because physically they would never be able to undertake the trip.

And so I say to my body, "Thanks for bringing me through."

Chapter 38
Santiago

We begin to get slap-happy. Other pilgrims warned us about this. Except it wasn't really a warning, it was more of a dreamy, enthused recounting of "those lovely last days when I walked 28 miles with my wonderful friends and I couldn't feel my toes by the end!! Haha. Isn't that cute?" *Haha*, the insanity of it all. Nicolas and I would look at each other sideways when people would tell us such anecdotes and assume a position of superiority. We are rational. We are educated. We are not inclined to make such a rash, impulsive decision.

But that was before Melide.

Melide is 35 miles from Santiago di Compostella. We weren't even planning to stop in Melide. The idea was to stop a the town before Melide and to walk on through it to Lavacolla the next day and arrive in Santiago the day after that.

Natalie and Mia sit next to us at a cafe as we're trying to plan the itinerary. We've been intersecting with our fellow walkers for a few days now, communicating through text messages and emails. It's the plan for everyone to meet up for a meal in Santiago, but as for sharing the road for the last two or three days, everyone sort of seems in a bubble, walking at the pace that they can manage. Marta is a day behind us. Robert and Célia are half a day ahead of us.

"We're thinking of walking through to Melide," says Natalie.

"Seriously? That's another 18 miles. That would put us ahead of Robert and Célia!"

"Yeah, but if we stop in Melide tonight, we'll arrive in Santiago two days earlier than planned."

Nic and I look at each other. Two days earlier. Are we ready for that? Is this what we want?

"We haven't reserved lodgings ..." Nic says unsurely.

I resist the temptation to roll my eyes. Nicolas has been well-planned, well-calculated and well-lodged throughout the entire trip. While most people told us it wasn't necessary to reserve space at Spanish hostels, Nic didn't like taking the chance and chose to call ahead every time he could.

I didn't want to harp on him on this point. Planning his itinerary obviously gave him a sense of security, and truth be told we'd had a good time of it as far as accommodations were concerned, so there was no reason to change his habits.

"I'm sure it'll be OK, hon. And being spontaneous will be good for you."

He pursed his lips at me.

"The question is whether or not we want our Camino to be done sooner than we thought," I say wistfully.

Nic motions to the cafe. "Jen, look around." There was literally not a free seat in the place. What with the influx of all the last-stretch walkers, the potential for road tension is obvious. The new pilgrims are hogging the trail, speaking loudly, partying at night and making rookie mistakes such as carrying too much weight or wearing bad footwear, which made them complain even louder.

They were in a different space than we were. The older lot of us had even concurred that we weren't up for meeting new people. We no longer had the energy for it. We looked for each other at cafes, bars and hostels at the end of the day and stuck together, eyeing down the newbies. It was part snobbism, part fatigue. We had found our beat, but now there were four or five times the number of people we were used to seeing on the road and it was creating a nervous shock for all of us. I was beginning to imitate Roman's sense of exasperation with the human race. Nic reads my thoughts.

"The Camino is over, at least the Camino as we know it. Right now, the idea is just to reach Santiago. We're not going to get the solace that we'd gotten used to anymore. Why not sprint it? Célia and Robert will be sprinting it too. We may even beat the crowds."

"My thoughts exactly," says Natalie, "Besides, Mark and the kids just arrived in Barcelona and I am aching to see my family."

"So Melide it is," I say.

"YEAH!!" Says Natalie in her best rocker chick voice, "Melide!!!"

And that's how Nicolas and I undertook our first 28 miles of walking in one day. It wasn't bad. I had some minor aches in my legs and a few feelings of wooziness, but in all I felt surprisingly good.

Or at least, the adrenaline felt good. I should have known the adrenaline was setting in from all the cokes I was drinking. Or when I began cheering on the cyclists who whizzed past us on the road, and who had up to now pissed me off because they nearly knocked me over every time. Now I was rejoicing in their existence which should have been an indicator of my waning state. Another indicator may have been during the last three miles when I couldn't feel my legs but kept on saying, "I feel GREAT!"

I ignored my cardinal rule: Listen to your body. Manuel, the innkeeper at Villatuerta had told us, this. Célia had demonstrated the importance of this lesson when she wound up at the emergency room after Burgos. And countless experienced pilgrims had repeated that mantra to me over the last 63 days. But I paid no attention. Actually it was worse than ignoring it; I forgot its very existence.

Which means that the next day, I repeated the same experience. We did our first 13 miles in no time at all. Stopped for coffee, ate a croissant, drank a little water. No problem.

Then we did another six miles. We flopped down on a chair and said hello to some familiar faces. Mia and Natalie pulled up a chair next to us. Nic pulled out a map. "You know what this means," he said, peering down at the book.

"What?"

"Another six miles and we can reach Santiago tomorrow."

"Wow." I thought for a minute. "It feels unreal. I wasn't counting on arriving in Santiago until two days from now. It's insane."

"Mark will not believe it," says Natalie.

"I can barely believe it myself!" I say to them, "Come on, let's go!"

And that's when I had my first out-of-body experience. It only lasted a fraction of a second. I didn't even mention it. But as I got up, I felt as if I left my body sitting on the chair behind me. As if my mind and my flesh separated. My legs felt heavy, my head woozy, and I had to lean on my walking poles so as not to topple over. Hmm, I thought, that's funny. And then it passed.

And still I didn't realize what I was doing to my body.

I didn't wake up and think that walking more than 44 miles in less than 48 hours was a dangerous thing to undertake. That I'd only had seven hours of sleep in this whole time. That I probably hadn't kept on top of my water intake. That I was on the verge of serious dehydration and muscular exhaustion. That was "wise Jenna's" diagnosis of the situation. Slap-happy, Jenna just kept on saying, " This is so cool ! I feel so great!"

We end our next six miles in a cafe. I bemoan the fact that there is no food. "We'll just have to eat when we get to our hotel," I say, sipping some water.

"Two more miles," says Nic.

"Let's do it."

We begin walking through a eucalyptus forest. The out-of-body thing happened again. This time, however, I felt myself tipping over. "This is strange," I thought to myself, "but I don't think I can stand up anymore."

"Nic !" I call out. And as I do, he turns around to see me collapse onto the ground. "Don't get up," I tell myself. "No problem," myself replied. "Have you noticed your limbs won't move?"

"Huh," I reply, as I try to bend my knee. "Look at that. It won't budge."

In the meantime, Nicolas is tearing towards me.

"Jen!" he gasps.

"I'm fine."

"You don't look it."

Natalie and Mia run up beside us. "Did you faint?" Mia asks.

"Not really ... I just couldn't hold myself up anymore."

"Come on." Nic pulls me up and takes my bag. "Let's see if we can get you to the next village. I'll walk with your bag."

"Oh, my goodness" fusses Natalie, "I can't believe we've walked so much. This was irresponsible ..."

"Hey, I'm thirty years old. I made my choices," I said comfortingly, thinking to myself that it really was so irresponsible of me. How could I have done this?

"Oh, my God," says Mia. "For a minute there, I thought you were going to be a Camino bench!"

"Mia, it is so not the time to bring that up!" cries Natalie.

Scattered along the road are memorial benches set up with commemorative plaques for various pilgrims who died along the Way. It is sort of a running gag that you have to take good care of yourself if you don't want to wind up a Camino bench. "It's OK Mia," I say. "I had the same thought."

We walk in silence, the four of us pondering the possibilities of my near and sudden death. What do we do if I collapse again? We're in a eucalyptus forest in Galicia. There can't be that many ambulances nearby. Nicolas keeps shooting me concerned glances.

"It's OK, Nic."

"I've never been so scared in my life."

I look at him, and realize he's telling the truth. "Honey," I say softly, feeling touched. He touches my hand and we keep walking.

To everyone's relief we make it to the hotel. I lie down on the bed, thinking, "This is OK, this is OK. I'll be fine tomorrow."

A few hours later I start throwing up.

Nicolas enters and sees me lying on the cold tile floor, with a washcloth over my face.

"Well at least it's out of your system."

"I'll say," I say feebly.

A few hours later, though, my body still hadn't had the last word. I run to the bathroom as I feel the last remains of the day's meals exit violently through my esophagus.

Nicolas, true to his routine, enters after me and pulls my hair back, mopping my forehead. I keep remembering a lecture my professor of theological anthropology gave once about the body, how some philosophers believe that the body has a will, a spirit, even a mind of its own, and that if you do not respect this being, it will answer back, revolt, shut down. I was living out the proof of that thesis. Right now my body was screaming insults and rage at my person, threatening it with more riots, more rebellions, more troublemaking. All I could do was beg it to quiet down and minimize the damages.

Nicolas tries to sweet talk me. "Well, now it's really out. You'll feel better soon."

He's wrong. My body is not yet in a spirit of negotiation. I throw up every hour, on the hour, for the rest of the night. By four in the morning I was dry heaving over the poor toilet bowl which had seen far too much action for one night. Nicolas, pale-faced and frightened, begins to look desperate.

"This has got to stop."

"You think?" I say hoarsely, panting on the floor.

"It must be food poisoning. What did you eat?"

I wrack my brain for what could have put me in this state. What is the spoonful of yogurt that tasted a bit off? The bottles of water filled from taps outside the farm house? The Danish that had sat a bit too long in my bag? The prawns I ate for supper? Or was it simply my body trying to rid itself of my own stupidity? Was a violent stomach sickness the best way to shake me awake from my irresponsibility?

In any case, we both agreed it was time to go to the hospital.

I knock on Natalie and Mia's door and tell them what's happened. Natalie, the ever-ready pilgrim-mom kicks into action, taking my temperature and giving me protein powder to mix with water while Nicolas calls a cab.

"I know in my heart of hearts that you are going to be OK," says Natalie. I don't know if she's saying that because it's true or if she's just reassuring my panicked self, but it works, and I feel myself calm down.

It's dark outside; dawn hasn't yet broken. The taxi pulls up and we tell him to take us to the hospital.

The taxi driver takes off at such a speed that I fear I'll lose my stomach once more, so I clutch the arm rest and hold on for dear life. What time the Spanish lose during siesta they make up for on the road. We pull up to the hospital and I drag myself inside. The waiting room is empty. Apparently no one is awake enough to be sick at this hour. The receptionist looks at us and gathers that we are pilgrims.

"Feet or stomach?" she asks. Obviously they have a long trail of *peregrinos* at their doors.

I explain to her in very broken Spanish what happened, acting out fainting and then throwing up "cinqo" times. She finds this most amusing and takes my Canadian Medicare card.

"Remind me to thank the health minister," I say to Nic when no bill is produced.

The doctor takes a quick look at me and to my dismay does not send me for X-rays, CT scans, ultrasounds, and blood and urine samples. She simply scribbles a couple of prescriptions and sends me on my way.

"What do you want?" Nic asks. "You've obviously got textbook something, either food poisoning or the flu. No use doing any tests when all you need is to rest and replenish your fluids."

"I want to leave the hospital feeling better. I don't," I say miserably.

Nic takes hold of my hand. "Come on." He hails another taxi cab. The taxi pulls into town and the driver opens the door. I can feel myself roll out of the car and be propped up on a stone bench which overlooks a square. I lift my feet onto the bench and use my bag as a pillow. I open my eyes and take in the sights around me.

We were in front of La Cathédrale de Santiago di Compostella.

Santiago

Chapter 39
Aftermath

It is said that the great warriors of legend will live through epic battles and death-defying experiences, barely surviving hunger, cold, misery and pain, only to declare when their adventures are over, that they long to experience more of the same.

Is this a commentary on the human condition? That we are eternally unsatisfied with the ordinary? That we cannot find contentment in the mundane or in simplicity? That we are actually happier in difficult situations than in easier ones?

It could be, of course, the amazing human ability to forget the pain and the misery when the outcome is so good and so happy. I have a friend who suffered a traumatic experience when she gave birth to her son. Her labor lasted 36 hours, was riddled with complications and finally resulted in an emergency C-section followed by six weeks of intensive recovery. Yet when she told us about it, she was rather serene: "It's true what they say. Objectively, I can tell that the whole shebang was the worst thing I'd ever gone through. But emotionally, I simply don't feel that bad about it. When Alex was finally born, everything was OK."

And that's how I feel about my arrival in Santiago di Compostella. Objectively, I remember the weeks of blisters, being haunted by Lucy and Bruce, and the pain in my knees and shins. I remember the days of icy rain, soaking me to the bone, and the scorching, searing sun beating down on my face. I remember the food poisoning and the discomfort at the hospital and in the taxi cab. But emotionally, I cannot connect with those memories. My memories upon arriving in Santiago and looking up at the Cathedral are those of overwhelming emotion. It was not just joy. It was not just relief. It was completion. My stomach was still raw, and my body so very weak. I could barely stand straight.

"Come on," says Nicolas determinedly. "I can't go to the credential office without you. I just can't."

Nicolas' voice is so emotional, so set. It is an "on your feet soldier!" moment. I wonder whether or not I'll be able to set my feet on the ground. I just feel so winded, weak and nauseous. My gut is telling me to cry for mercy and tell him to go on without me. But I look into my husband's face and I realize that if I did that, I would hurt him. I need to finish this with him.

"OK," I say feebly. And so I get up and walk with him down the street, holding my shoulders.

"Careful. My skin hurts."

"All right. Just one step after another. Look, the office is here."

We arrive at the stone house and step into the courtyard. It had barely opened. It's still the earliest hours of the morning, but already there is a line of pilgrims forming, all smiling in their haggard, ragged states, smelling up to the high heavens, pasted with dirt and dust from days on the road.

A mother and daughter turn to us.

"We've seen you every now and then on stops on the road. When did you start out?"

"On the 12th of May," replied Nic.

The mother gasped. "My, but that's twice as long as most people here! You must have started out in France." We nod.

"This is my fourth Camino. I've done the ones in Portugal and the Via Plata as well. But it's my daughter's first."

"We've had very good experiences with mother-daughter teams," I say.

"Congratulations!" Nic says to the daughter and she beams at us.

"Are you all right?" she asks me, as I slump down on a step.

I tell her what happened. "The taxi drove us into Santiago just 40 minutes ago."

She smiled pityingly. "Don't you feel bad about it. The hospital is an entirely valid stage in the pilgrim's journey. It definitely counts."

I laugh. Ouch. It hurts to laugh. "Thanks. That makes me feel better. They should have stamps for our passports in the emergency room."

"Indeed."

We slowly make our way up the wooden stairs, with Nicolas carrying both our bags and holding me up by the shoulders. We finally get to the long desk where several well-organized volunteers are waiting to fill out the papers. Country, starting point, date of departure, fill out your names, why did you do the Camino? (There's that why question again.) Was it for religious, cultural, or religious-and-cultural reasons? Easy. We marked the third category.

We leave the rank-smelling office—there really is a distinct pilgrim smell—feeling bad that we hadn't offered the volunteers a facemask to block the odor or at least an incense burner or something.

I can feel my stomach settling, but it begins cramping up, no doubt from the lack of fluid, proteins, electrolytes and whatever else it may need to regain some sense of balance. My legs feel the cobblestones that are holding them up. The stones are so uneven that I wobble as I walk.

The streets are still empty, the town still asleep. We begin to make our way back to the main square. I feel tears pour down my face.

"Oh, Jen. Does everything still hurt?" Nicolas says concerned.

"No. Nothing hurts. We're here." He smiles at me, and in that unique moment, we truly understood each other.

After two months and more of trying to meet each other in our different paces, styles, needs, rhythms, our approaches to people and places, my shortcomings on the physical side, his shortcomings on the patience side, our spats about money, we finally saw each other, totally and completely. There was no one else but us; like wartime buddies, we knew what each other felt. Someone could have taken our hearts and melded them together: We could not have been more bonded. My beautiful husband, who made me stand and walk even though I wanted to lie down and feel sorry for myself.

Nicolas goes to get me my prescription at the pharmacy down the road. I lie back down on my bench, holding our credentials, crying softly for all I had behind me and for all I had acquired.

A few hours later, I greet Natalie and Mia. Natalie, sobbing, takes me in her arms and tells me she knew that I'd be all right. Then she introduces me to her husband, her two other children, whom she called "the littles," her mother and her aunt. I hug each one of them, hard and long, so very un-Canadian of me.

Looking back, I think I was using them as my own surrogate family. I wanted my mother, my father, my sisters and aunts to be there to hug me for what I had accomplished. In hugging Natalie's mother, I was hugging my own mother.

Then I hug Célia. I look at her drawn, wan face and compare it to earlier photos of her when we were in France, when she was colorful and plump, and realize how much she had aged. And yet she is happy, fulfilled, and full of ideas for her retirement.

"I will learn English," she says. "I will travel. And spend time with my grandchildren."

This woman, twice my age, had out-walked me many a day and still found the energy to nurse my bedbug bites and blisters. She'd freed herself from being under the corporate thumb and had finally made some life plans for herself, her own, very personal and independent life plans.

We would also meet up with Marta, who'd had a significantly more peaceful entrance into the city than me. Marta would continue on to Finistere on the Atlantic coast, about three days from Santiago. "I can see the appeal," I say to her, laughing, "but based on last night's experience, I'd say my Camino was over."

We would see a few people that we hadn't seen for weeks. I emailed Kit, Jane, Yan, Ann and Nadine, telling them all about my entrance into Santiago. I would be grateful for every person I see, knowing they were as much a part of my road as the cobblestones, the churches, the fields of lily flowers, the cows, the inns. I'm even grateful for the cathedral, as it provides a hub for final reunions. And I feel gratitude for Nicolas, who saw me through and who I now see with my own two eyes, just as he is, flawed and hilarious and perfect.

But for the moment, it is still the early hours of the morning, and I'm alone in the quiet of the square. Nicolas is a few streets down, getting my medicine. One solitary man sits in the center of the square, still wearing his backpack, facing the cathedral. For a very long time, I lie on the bench, crying until I could cry no more, while the man sits facing the church. He is in his world and I am in mine. Separate and yet together somehow.

Aftermath

Postlude
I Walked

We said goodbye to our fellow pilgrims, Célia and Marta and company, and Nicolas and I spent a few nights at Natalie's house in Barcelona, gently recuperating. "If you're still looking for a career move, you could always open a pilgrims' rehab center!" I joke with her. And then, finally, we head home.

It felt good to be home. "There are three journeys when you go to Compostelle," we were told. "The first is the planning. The second, the actual pilgrimage. The third, when you come back and relive the trip in your mind." The third voyage began when I got home, revisiting my walk, its memories and experiences.

The search for my Camino question was over. I had found my question. It was: What will I learn? My answer: Whatever you will allow the road to teach you. In fact, the hardest part, that which occupies my entire third Camino journey, is how to apply all of its lessons. There has been nothing instantaneous, no life-changing miracle, no clear revelation. There have simply been reflections, casting my mind back to the experiences, the conversations. And the writing.

I am still in my third journey. Maybe I will be for the rest of my life. The memories of the Camino are sometimes very vivid, sometimes vague, but I know that everything I learned about time, pacing one's self, choices, prayer and the body are still with me.

I walked. I walked through scorching sun and freezing rain, on feet that couldn't beat out the blisters, in a body that was faulty and imperfect, with feelings of being out of control. I walked with people I loved and I walked with strangers. I walked alone. I lived with my stress, and then I quieted my thoughts. I walked through beautiful places and talked about wonderful things. I walked in peace, and I walked in pain. Most of the time, the only lesson to be learned was that I needed to keep on walking.

I walked with my husband. We were, for the most part, like an unhinged pair of train wheels, whose coupling rod wasn't properly installed. His legs are long, mine are short. He is planned, I am less so. I remembered people's names. He asked me to remember them for him. And in our clumsiness, we found each other's pace. He walked, I walked.

We walked.

About Jenna Smith

Jenna Smith was born and raised in Montreal. She holds a masters degree in theology from Université de Montréal and was awarded the Dean's Prize for her thesis in 2011. She is the founding director of Innovation Youth, an inner city centre for teens and their families, offering education, life skills and community development services. When she's not leaving a trail of cookbooks and yarn behind her, you can usually find her biking on her way to the community garden.

About ULP

Urban Loft Publishers focuses on ideas, topics, themes, and conversations about all things urban. Renewing the city is the central theme and focus of what we publish. It is our intention to blend urban ministry, theology, urban planning, architecture, urbanism, stories, and the social sciences, as ways to drive the conversation. We publish a wide variety of urban perspectives, from books by the experts about the city to personal stories and personal accounts of urbanites (like Jenna!) who live in the city.

Made in the USA
Charleston, SC
28 April 2014